LITERACY INSTRUCTION IN MEXICO

by
Robert Miller

Phi Delta Kappa
International Studies in Education

We can only see in a picture what our experience permits us to see.

Edgar Dale

The Phi Delta Kappa International Studies in Education Series was established as a way to enlarge the common experience of education by publishing studies that bring to readers knowledge of heretofore unfamiliar theories, philosophies, and practices in the profession of education.

As the interdependence of nations becomes increasingly evident and necessary with the passage of time, so too must our understandings about education become shared property. In this sharing, we come increasingly to comprehend one another across civilizations and cultures, for education is at the core of human endeavor. Through education we pass on to succeeding generations not merely the accumulated wisdom of our past but the vision and means to create the future.

Literacy Instruction in Mexico is the ninth monograph in this series.

Previous titles:
Elementary Teacher Education in Korea
Teacher Education in the People's Republic of China
Innovation in Russian Schools
Changing Traditions in Germany's Public Schools
German Higher Education: Issues and Challenges
French Elementary Education and the Ecole Moderne
Education in the United Kingdom and Ireland
Care for Young Children in Four English-Speaking Countries

INTERNATIONAL STUDIES
IN EDUCATION

LITERACY INSTRUCTION IN MEXICO

by
Robert Miller

PHI DELTA KAPPA
EDUCATIONAL FOUNDATION
Bloomington, Indiana
U.S.A.

Cover design by
Peg Caudell

Library of Congress Control Number 2002113515
ISBN 0-87367-843-5

ACKNOWLEDGMENTS

I gratefully acknowledge the support of the International Relations Department of the Secretaría de Educación Pública in Mexico. Without their help, this project would not have been possible. I also want to acknowledge the hundreds of educators and government officials who answered questions, let me observe in their classrooms, and helped me in my quest to understand the Mexican system of education. The Mexicans have worked very hard to improve the education system in their country, and they have my profound respect.

I would like to acknowledge the help and guidance of Dr. Juan José Serrato Velasco, director of Bilateral Relations. His insight was extremely valuable. I would also like to thank the East Side Union High School District in San Jose, California, for granting three sabbaticals over 20 years so that I could pursue this investigation.

TABLE OF CONTENTS

INTRODUCTION

Literacy Instruction in Mexico is about my 20 years of research documenting the evolution of a school system through the 1970s, 1980s, and 1990s and discusses the proposed changes for the first six years of the current decade. Widespread discontent among teachers and administrators forced a major revision of the entire curriculum in 1972, and for the next 20 years the Secretaría de Educación Pública (SEP) made improvements to the basic system. The implementation of this new plan started in 1992. As we move into the 21st century, minor modifications of the 1992 plan will occur.

During the first school visit of the 20th year of my investigation, I asked the director of a primary school to tell me what would help teachers in the United States to understand the Mexican students in their classrooms. She replied, "We Mexicans have particular ideas about the world; we value truth, demand respect, honor, and we want to be consulted about things that concern us. Also, we have strong feelings about our country, our flag, our national hymn, and our history."[1] These elements, like the threads of an exotic tapestry, are woven throughout the Mexican education system. The reader will learn how Mexico reduced its illiteracy rate from 66% to 10% in less than 80 years and how it now provides schooling for almost 30 million people. As the chapters in this book focus on literacy in the primary schools, bilingual literacy instruction, adult literacy programs, special education and literacy, and the efforts to improve the quality of teachers, the themes of truth, respect, and nationalism will be evident.

Since 1978 I have been studying the education system of Mexico and examining ways that we can incorporate their ideas in the United States to help Mexican and Mexican-American stu-

1

dents succeed in school. The original study began during the 1978-79 school year. I studied official documents, interviewed officials from the SEP, and then wrote a description of the system and the process of teaching literacy. Of course, as any good educator knows, official descriptions are very different from the day-to-day survival strategies used in the schools. To balance the official description, I asked the SEP to recommend 30 schools in different parts of Mexico City. I devised a questionnaire for the teachers in the schools, observed one class in each school, and interviewed both the director and the teachers of the schools. In all, I collected 300 completed questionnaires from the teachers, observed in 26 classrooms for a total of 23 hours, and interviewed 26 teachers and directors. All of this research provided a more precise view of the Mexican school system (and a doctoral dissertation). In 1989, 10 years after the first study, I visited 12 of the original schools, gave questionnaires to the teachers, observed in classes, and interviewed both the teachers and the directors. During September and October of 1998, I replicated the complete study.

Over the past 20 years I made 13 visits to Mexico, analyzed 632 questionnaires, visited more than 100 schools, interviewed the directors and selected teachers in these schools, visited 70 classrooms, and spoke with more than 100 officials in various agencies of the Mexican government. Besides Mexico City, I visited schools and other education facilities in the states of Jalisco, Oaxaca, México, Guanajuato, and Michoacán. During the summer of 2001, I went back to Mexico to chart the changes in the system since the end of the study. I interviewed three school directors and officials in the SEP.

Most Mexicans entering the United States are not from Mexico City. However, the money for the schools, the model of education, the textbooks, the curriculum, and the teacher training programs all emanate from Mexico City. The educational materials, curricula, and practices in the states are the same as in Mexico City.

This book, inspired by the United Nations Educational, Scientific, and Cultural Organization (UNESCO) studies of William S.

Gray and the comparative reading studies by John Downing,[2] contains the results of my work, and all of the ideas and opinions are the product of my views on Mexican education. I realize that factors outside the influence of the education system overpower learning, and the *potential* for success is greater than the actual achievements. These factors include hunger, homelessness, drug abuse, divorce, and violence. Although these negative factors are present, this book focuses on the positive values and achievements of the Mexican education system.

There are constant reminders that the Mexican system is not perfect. I entered a restaurant in Mexico City at 6:30 a.m. It was raining; and on the cold cement sidewalk under the overhang by the front window, two school-age boys were asleep. This is a reminder that, though Mexico has made great progress, there are still people who receive little or no education. There is a very large population of children who work on the streets of Mexico City. Estimates are that this population exceeds 13,000 children.[3] In the suburbs of Mexico City there are not enough schools, and members of the Chamber of Deputies (congress) have noted that the poorer states of Oaxaca, Michoacán, Veracruz, and Guerrero need more and better-trained teachers for their indigenous populations.[4]

Many immigrants to the United States are from the poorer states, and this provides a distorted view of the accomplishments of the Mexican education system. The average of the states shows that 85% of the students complete the six years of primary school. However, this number is 66% for Chiapas, 75% for Oaxaca, 77% for Guerrero, 78% for Michoacán, and 79% for Yucatán. The number is more than 95% for Baja California, Tlaxcala, Mexico City, and Baja California Sur. It is more than 90% for the states of Sonora, Hidalgo, México, Aguascalientes, Coahuila, Quintana Roo, Morelos, Nuevo León, and Querétaro.[5]

It is important to examine the history of the school system to place Mexico's achievements in context. Education was not a priority in Mexico during the period of Spanish rule. The first revolution against the Spanish occurred in 1810. It failed, and finally in 1824 Mexico became a republic. In 1846 there was a war between Mexico and the United States, and in 1857 Mexico plunged into a civil war. By 1860 there was peace.

The Catholic Church operated most of the schools before 1857. Wherever there was a church, there was a school. The most successful secular school system existing within the country was the tutorial system devised by Lancaster, an Englishman, that lasted from 1824 to 1890. Only 11 of these schools existed in the entire country: four for boys, five for girls, one co-educational, and one night school for adults. Each of these schools had one teacher and educated approximately 600 students.[6] The teacher trained students, called "monitors," and, in turn, the monitors trained the other students.

During the presidency of Benito Juárez (1858-1872), the federal government took over all of the possessions of the church, including the schools. Education at this point became a function of the state. In the constitution of 1857, free and compulsory schooling became the law. The family, the municipality, the state, and the various religious organizations ran the schools; and there was no change until 1921. In 1871 there were 8,103 primary schools. Only one-fifth of the population received a primary school education.[7]

Several factors shaped the national school system. After Juárez took power from the church in 1859, Mexico began to develop a secular philosophy of education. Ignacio Ramírez, an intellectual and member of Juárez's cabinet, suggested the reorganization of the curriculum into three parts. In the first part there were courses in gymnastics, living languages, singing, reading, writing, musical notes, arithmetic, algebra, and geometry. The second part consisted of historical studies, including truth, beauty, literature, and law. Laboratories for natural history, physics, and chemistry constituted the third aspect of the program.[8]

Under the influence of Ramírez, Dr. Gabino Barreda, who was in charge of secondary education, instituted the new philosophy of "positivism." This philosophy held that mathematical reasoning was the basis of a scientific education, and this was the only way to arrive at valid knowledge. Biology, physiology, physics, and chemistry became the basic subjects of education. Classical language study was severely limited. The study of history and literature received little time. Sociology replaced philosophy as a subject of study.

In 1891, because of the driving leadership of Justo Sierra, government education programs took form. Sierra, who first accepted "positivism" and then rejected it, tended to stress moral precepts over scientific investigation. Sierra was an exceptional individual who served as a member of the Chamber of Deputies, a magistrate in the supreme court, assistant secretary of public instruction, and the organizer of the national university. Sierra created one primary school for every 1,000 students.

During fiscal year 1905-06, the government spent 1.9 million pesos on primary education in the Federal District and in the territories. By 1910, this amount increased to 3.9 million pesos. In spite of these expenditures, the statistics for 1910 show that:

- More than two-thirds of the total population of 15,139,855 could neither read nor write.
- Less than one-fourth of the school-age population was enrolled in school.
- School conditions in the Federal District (Mexico City) were far superior to those in the states and territories, and schooling in the rural area (where over two-thirds of the population lived) was almost completely neglected.[9]

The foundation for the current system began in 1911 with the overthrow of the Porfiro Diaz regime. A system of rural schools, developed primarily for the Indian populations and independent of the primary schools, was formed between 1911 and 1917. These rural schools represented a significant policy change. For the first time, the federal government assumed some responsibility for education outside the Federal District. By 1924, a network of 1,089 rural schools was served by 1,146 teachers and administered by 48 inspector-instructors.[10] Also, approximately 1,000 traveling libraries were in service.

The Constitution of 1917 also stated several significant policies. It made instruction free and secular, and it disallowed religious

5

entities from establishing primary schools unless the schools were subject to official supervision.

The federal education movement gained momentum in 1921 with the appointment of José Vasconcelos as the Secretary of Public Education. Vasconcelos said, "What this country needs is to sit down and read the Iliad. I am going to distribute a hundred thousand Homers in the schools of the nation and in the libraries we are going to set up." When peasant families acquired inexpensive editions of the classics — Dante, Homer, Cervantes, and Tolstoy — they displayed them close to the altar or in another prominent place in their homes.[11]

Vasconcelos believed that education should lift the individual in a spiritual and intellectual sense, and he developed a curriculum that stressed philosophy, art, religion, morals, and the classics. He also believed that the peasant families should speak Spanish instead of their native languages. The government established more than 1,000 rural schools, opened popular libraries, and widely distributed agricultural, classical, and manual training books by 1924.

In 1924 José Manuel Puig Casaurac succeeded Vasconcelos. Puig's closest ally was Moisés Sáenz, a Mexican educator who studied under John Dewey at Columbia University. He sponsored a version of Dewey's action school, in which the teacher becomes a community leader as much as a classroom instructor. Under Sáenz, rural schools expanded; and he sought a more practical focus for the schools than did Vasconcelos.

Rural normal schools were first established in 1926. These schools were dedicated to the task of preparing the children of peasants for teaching positions among peasants. This is the historical precedent for the current program of *promotores*.

Anti-illiteracy campaigns started in the 1920s. A sweeping effort to have "each one teach one" produced observable results. The campaign of 1944-46 saw the printing and distribution of 10 million *cartillas* (reading primers) and workbooks. A phonetic approach became the preferred method in books published for adults.[12]

From 1946 to 1952, the government built 5,069 new primary schools in addition to the 12,000 already existing, and they built 2,606 more from 1952-58. Today more than 200,000 primary schools exist in Mexico.

In June of 1957 the Consejo Nacional Técnico de la Educación was created to unify instructional services and to examine programs of study, texts, and education organizations. (It is now called Consejo Nacional Técnico de la Educación, or CONALTE.) In 1959 the SEP requested the Consejo "to study and revise the elementary curriculum so that it would contribute more to the growth of civic responsibility and practical skills."[13] The revised curriculum was organized according to six functions: 1) protect health and improve physical fitness, 2) promote study of the physical environment and of the conservation of natural resources, 3) create understanding of the social life and improve social life, 4) teach creative activities, 5) teach practical activities, and 6) develop the elements of culture.[14]

The government printed the first official textbook in 1960.[15] By 1964 the government issued 114 million textbooks. In 1998-99, 147 million books for primary and secondary schools were distributed.[16] These books were given to the primary school children free of charge.

The Educación Para Todos program tried to increase the services of the primary school, teach Spanish, and provide education for adults between 1978-82. This program ended, and the adult education program (INEA) continued these goals. Currently, the illiteracy rate is 10%. INEA is in charge of adult education, and there is a continuous drive to increase literacy. INEA also encourages businesses to have literacy programs by providing free materials. The businesses pay for the teachers.

One program of note is for the military. During his 18th year, a male must spend every Saturday doing military service. Young men who cannot read are tutored by those who have a primary or secondary school education.[17]

Seven million Mexicans speak indigenous languages. To meet their needs, the Department of Indian Affairs was created in

1978. The department provides bilingual schools, bilingual textbooks (for primary schools and adult education), *albergues escolares* (boarding schools), *escullas albergues* (bilingual boarding schools), and cultural missions. Bilingual textbooks are in 46 languages or dialects for the primary schools. INEA also has bilingual textbooks for adults.

Centros de Educación Initial are offered for families with children aged birth to four years. Albergues escolares and escullas albergues offer dormitories, where the students live from Monday to Friday; the students go back to their villages on the weekend. Cultural missions teach trades, educate the indigenous peoples on health issues, and teach literacy. In communities with fewer than 100 people, teachers visit to educate the children.[18]

It is impractical to have large high schools in rural areas. Instead, they use television programs from Mexico City, transmitted by satellite. The programs last 15 minutes, and the students work on the lesson for 35 minutes under the supervision of a secondary school teacher. Seven subjects are taught in a six-hour day. There are eight books for the first year, eight for the second, and 12 for the third. The department has created 4,600 programs at a cost of $5,000 (in U.S. dollars) per program. Other countries using the video from the satellite and the workbooks are Costa Rica, Panama, El Salvador, Guatemala, the Dominican Republic, Nicaragua, and Honduras.[19]

From 1972-1993 the primary method of teaching reading was the *metódo global* (a whole language approach with structural analysis), and changes in the curriculum aimed at refining this method. The first- and second-grade curriculum integrated skills, and all of the subjects in these years were taught in thematic units.

The Salinas administration (1988-1994) decided to change Mexico. Their initial actions included a free-trade agreement with the United States and Canada that reduced bureaucracy so that foreigners would invest in Mexico and stabilize the economy. In May 1992 they made the decision to change the education system. The new curriculum went into effect in September 1992 and stressed science and math. Also, instructional methods in the primary schools reverted to the models used before 1972 (the date of the last major change in education). Finally, they decided to decentralize education by turning all facilities outside Mexico City over to the states. The school system as of 1992-93 included federal schools in the Distrito Federal (Mexico City) and state schools. However, all decisions concerning curriculum, courses, textbooks, and programs were made in Mexico City.

In 1996, Ernesto Zedillo became president of Mexico. He had held several positions in the Salinas cabinet, one of which was Secretary of Education. The decentralization of the education system continued under his leadership. New textbooks were developed, teachers used different methods for primary reading instruction, and education budgets increased.

Over the 20 years of this study, the number of students completing the six years of the *primaria* has improved. At the end of the 1981-82 academic year, 62% of the students completed the *primaria*; and 85% completed it in 1997-98. However, the completion rate still is a problem; and the SEP has many programs designed to increase this percentage.

In December 2000 Vincente Fox became the new president of Mexico. Rafael Rangel Sostmann, the head of the education transitional team, indicated that the new president would support and continue the programs of the previous president. Their goals focus on extending the benefits of education to everyone, improving the current schools, and improving the system of education.

There was excitement when I talked to the directors about the first new program proposed by the current administration. The program is called *Escuelas de Calidad* (quality schools). Qualifying schools will receive 100,000 pesos to be used for construction and repair of the facilities and for a broad range of things that support learning and teaching activities. To qualify for the money, the schools had to prepare and submit a proposal before 21 September 2001. During the week of June 18-22, school directors in Mexico City attended workshops on how to write the proposals. The proposals included an evaluation of the current conditions of the school and a plan to improve the quality of the education services that the school provides. The parents of the students also had to be included in the plan. If a school is accepted, at least 60% of the money will be used for constructing classrooms, purchasing furniture, or purchasing equipment. Twenty percent will be used for repair and renovation of the school, and the rest can be used for learning and educational activities. Under no circumstances can the money be used to pay teachers or directors. Funds were provided to 2,240 schools in 2001-2002 and to 9,447 schools in 2002-2003.

One major change in Mexican society will have a profound effect on the schools. Thirty percent of women used birth control in 1976; now 70% do so. Families in the mid-1960s had an average of 7.2 children; now that figure is 2.4 and is predicted to decline to 2.1 by 2005. The primary school population, ages six to 11, will decline by 3% during the current administration and by 10% by the end of the first decade of this century.[20] This change will allow the government to focus more on the quality of education.

This short history of the Mexican school system reveals the incredible amount of progress made to develop a modern education system. Education is about the search for truth, and in Mexico this search started from a religious base. The Catholic Church administered all the schools. Then the search for truth in secular society began. Mathematical reasoning became the basis for finding truth, and the changes brought about a definition of truth that stressed philosophy, morals, and the classics. A pragmatic approach followed, and now the new curriculum is, again, using science and mathematics as the tools for finding truth. Nationalism also has emerged in the period since 1921 when the federal education movement began. The leaders of the country have the education of all Mexicans as a goal and have assumed responsibility for education outside Mexico City.

From these beginnings came the powerful Secretaría de Educación Pública, which provides all public education and monitors private education in Mexico. How is this bureaucracy organized and what type of services does it provide to the people of Mexico? Chapter One begins the exploration to answer this question. In Chapter Two I take up basic literacy, moving to special literacy in Chapter Three and special education in Chapter Four. In Chapter Five I focus on teacher education. Chapter Six deals with Spanish literacy for Mexicans in the United States. Finally, in Chapter Seven I consider some of the likely future trends in Mexican education.

Notes

1. Maria Cristina Rodriquez Ramirez, Directora, Escuela Primaria "Estado de Hidalgo" 11-0515, 22 September 1998.
2. William S. Gray, *The Teaching of Reading and Writing* (Paris: UNESCO, 1956); John Downing, *Comparative Reading: Cross National Studies of Behavior and Processes in Reading and Writing* (New York: Macmillian, 1973).
3. Molly Moore, "Mexican Waifs Ply Meanest of Streets," *Washington Post*, 10 December 1996, p. A1.
4. The Chamber of Deputies held a debate on this subject on Wednesday, 24 September 1998.
5. *Compendio Estadístico-Gráfico de Educación, 1997* (Mexico: Instituto Nacional de Estadística Geografía e Informática, 1998).
6. Evelyn Blair, "Educational Movements in Mexico, 1821 to 1836," doctoral dissertation, University of Texas, 1941, p. 316.
7. Irma Wilson, *Mexico: A Century of Educational Thought* (Greenwood, Conn.: Greenwood Press, 1974), p. 206.
8. Ibid., p. 201.
9. Clark Gill, *Education in a Changing Mexico* (Washington, D.C.: U.S. Government Printing Office, 1969), p. 20.
10. Ibid., p. 23.
11. Stanley Ivie, "A Comparison in Educational Philosophy: Jose Vasconcelos and John Dewey," *Comparative Education Review* 10 (October 1966): 404.
12. Mary Joan Leonard, "Anti-Illiteracy Campaigns in Mexico, 1944-46," master's thesis, University of California at Berkeley, 1958, p. 61.

13. *Education in a Changing Mexico*, p. 38.
14. Ibid.
15. Vincent Padget, *The Mexican Political System* (Atlanta, Ga.: Houghton-Mifflin, 1976), p. 206.
16. *Comisión Nacional de los Libros de Texto Gratuitos.* http://www.conaliteg.gob.mx/cuadro1998.html.
17. *Instituto Nacional Para la Educación de los Adultos, Marco Operativo del Programa* (Mexico: Secretaría de Educación, 1997).
18. Interview with Lic. Jose Carmen Díaz Miguel, DGEI, in Mexico City, 15 October 1998.
19. Interview with Lic. Natanael Carro Bello and Lic. Guadalupe Fuentes Cardova, *Telesecundaria* program, in Mexico City, 15 October 1998.
20. James Smith, "Changing Demographics Create Opportunities for Fox," *The News*, Mexico City, 24 September 2000. http://www.novedades.com.mx /national.htm.

CHAPTER ONE

THE SCHOOL SYSTEM: AN OVERVIEW

A visitor to the Plaza of Three Cultures in Tlataloco, in the northern part of Mexico City, first observes an Aztec ruin, complete with a stone altar and signs explaining the various Aztec structures. Next to this ruin is a 16th century colonial church built by the Spaniards. Surrounding the area are condominiums and modern office buildings.

The Plaza of Three Cultures is an appropriate symbol for the three forces shaping Mexico's education system. First, the Aztec ruin represents the indigenous peoples. Mexico has more than seven million indigenous peoples, and they are the poorest of all Mexicans.

Second, the colonial church represents the repressive rule of the Spaniards and the authoritarianism that has plagued Mexico through the centuries. It is an especially appropriate symbol because of its more recent history. Around 5:30 p.m. on 2 October 1968, about 10,000 people were gathered in front of the church to protest the massive amount of money the government spent on the 1968 Olympic Games in Mexico City. Soldiers hidden in the ruins began firing, and hundreds of secret police agents began making arrests. The bodies were carried away in the night, and firetrucks washed away the blood. The government claimed that 32 people had died, but a more probable number was between 200 and 300.[1] Each year on October 2, there is a student march to force the government to open the records to the public.

And third are the modern office buildings, symbol of the Information Age. The forces of this modern age are a direct contrast to the authoritarian system. Decisions now are made in many locations, and knowledge is power.

The interaction of these three forces is central to understanding the Mexican education system.

The System of Education

Mexican education begins with the *preescolar* for students age four to six. The preescolar is voluntary. At age six, students enter the *primaria* and attend for six years, until age 12. Students continuing to the university will attend the *secundaria* for three years and a *media superior* school for three years. For some occupations, the secundaria serves as a trade school. The next level is the *superior*, which refers to teacher-training schools and universities, including post-graduate work.

The largest part of the school system is the primaria, enrolling 55.9% of all students in the late 1990s. At the end of the decade, 11.3% of the students were enrolled in preescolar, 17.1% in the secundaria, 9.5% in media superior, and 6.2% in superior education.[2] The three years of secundaria has been considered to be part of basic education since the early 1990s, and the goal is for all Mexicans to be educated to this level. However, in 1998-99 there were 14.6 million students enrolled in federal, state, and private primarias and only five million students enrolled in the secundaria.[3]

After a student completes the six years of the primaria, he or she enrolls in the secundaria for three more years. The secundaria level contains several options. Students can enroll in a general program, a vocational program, a program for working people, or in the *telesecundaria* program offered through television. Students in the general secundaria will enter a profession. The vocational secundaria offers industrial, agricultural, forestry, or marine training. Finally, students in rural areas and small towns often are educated in the telesecundaria. The proportion of students in the different types of secundaria is as follows: general secundaria 51%, technical programs 29%, telesecundaria 19%, and secundarias for workers 1%. Since 1982 a movement to build secundarias has resulted in dramatic increases in the number of schools. In 1978-79 there were only 7,711 secundarias in the country. By June 1998 there were 26,745 secundarias.[4] Of this total, 958 were federal, 22,798 were state, and 2,989 were private.[5]

Teachers have several options to receive the training necessary to work in the secundaria. Those planning a career in the secundaria can attend the primaria, secundaria, media superior, and then the *normal superior.* Those teachers who work in the primaria can attend the normal superior, or the Universidad Nacional Pedagógica (UPN) to specialize in a subject taught in the secundaria. Many primary school teachers also work in the secundaria. In the 1989 survey given to teachers, about 14% of the primary school teachers said they also worked in the secundaria.

The classes in the secundaria are 50 minutes long, and the teachers rotate between the classes. Students take Spanish, mathematics, natural science, biology, physics, chemistry, social science, geography, history, civics, and a foreign language for all

Table 1. Subjects and time spent per week in the secundaria.

Subject	Grade 1	Grade 2	Grade 3
Spanish	5	5	5
Mathematics	5	5	5
World History	3	3	
History of Mexico			3
General Geography	3		
Geography of Mexico		2	
Educational Orientation			3
Civics	3	2	
Elective			3
Biology	3	2	
Introduction to Physics and Chemistry	3		
Physics		3	3
Chemistry		3	3
Foreign Language	3	3	3
Artistic Expression	2	2	2
Physical Education	2	2	2
Technology	3	3	3
Total	35	35	35

Source: *Plan y Programas de Estudio (secundaria),* p. 15.

three years of the secundaria. Table 1 shows a roster of these subjects and the amount of time the typical student spends each week studying them.

I visited General Francisco Villa Escuela Secundaria in Mexico City in 1983. First-year English students were studying possessives. Using the teaching method typically found in Mexico, the teacher wrote different items on the board, and the students copied them in their notebooks.

In a second-year English class the students were reviewing the structure of English. Each student stood and answered the questions in English. In a third-year Spanish class, the teacher was reviewing regular and irregular verbs. Students stood up and recited the answers to the questions. After the drills, the students copied the information into their notebooks. In 1982 this secundaria had the highest graduation rate in Mexico City, about 83%. Teachers indicated that between 70% and 80% of the students graduated from an average secundaria. Official statistics for the nation from the 1997-98 school year (15 years later) showed a graduation rate of 89.8%.[6]

As part of the official modernization curriculum, the teaching of English focuses on a student's fluency through the use of role-playing and task-based instruction, instead of correcting grammatical mistakes. However, these methods are not common in the Mexican schools. Many teachers of English can read and write English, but their oral English skills are deficient.

There are other aspects to the modernization program for the secundaria. The curriculum for the first year of the secundaria was rewritten in September 1992. This curriculum included history, geography, and civics. Also, the number of hours spent studying Spanish and mathematics increased. Areas no longer are the focus; instead, the focus is specific subjects within the area. In mathematics, for example, reasoning and estimation are emphasized.

Besides the general secundarias, there are several types of vocational secundarias. These include secundarias for workers and those for industrial, agricultural, and forestry training. In addition, there are secundarias for marine training and bilingual secundarias.

In rural areas, books and television programs help the people learn. During the 1997-98 school year, Mexico had 14,101 telesecundarias serving 890,400 students.[7] The broadcasts originate in Mexico City and are sent over the Solidaridad satellites. The telesecundaria provides a cheaper alternative to the regular secondary school. With this program there is only one teacher per class, rather than the several specialized teachers found in the regular secundaria. The schools are small, and each room has a television set. Programs are professionally produced using actors in Mexico City. Each program lasts 15 minutes, and the students use workbooks for the other 35 minutes of a typical class. At exactly 8:03 a.m. the first program of the day begins with the mathematics lesson for the first year of secondary school. Broadcast of the mathematics lesson for the second year occurs 15 minutes later. Finally, 15 minutes later the third-year program begins. The order for the courses is mathematics, Spanish, natural science, social science, English, art, technological education, and physical education. There are 176 lessons divided into eight units.

I visited a telesecundaria in Oaxaca in October 1998. The school was on a country road, and it looked like a typical elementary school — about five classrooms, a basketball court, and a director's office. The satellite dish on top of the school indicated that it was a telesecundaria. The classrooms were dark, and the 30 or so students in each room were staring at two 26-inch color television sets. On the monitor, the actors were describing an aspect of biology. The objectives were listed at the beginning of the lesson. The setting for the lesson on biology was in a field so that the students could understand the practical application of the material being studied. After the concept was taught, there was a review. The lesson ended after 15 minutes. The instructors used the television program as the introduction to the subject and then taught the students using textbooks, student notebooks, and the chalkboard.

Upon completing the secundaria, students move to the media superior level. These schools focus on students aged 15 to 18; and

17

when the students finish, they have the *bachillerato*, which is equivalent to a high school diploma. Approximately 58% of the graduates of the secundaria in 1997-98 enrolled in the general bachillerato program. The object of this program is to prepare the students to continue their studies and to enter the university or the normal school. This program focuses on developing the character of the students, basic education, scientific thought, and language instruction.

For the general bachillerato, students have the option of either attending school or using the open *preparatoria* program on television. In the open preparatoria, students study at their own pace and can take as long as they need to complete the requirements.

About 28% of the students are in the *bachillerato tecnologico* program. This course of study has two functions: the students can go directly to work after receiving the degree or they can opt to study technical fields at the university. As of August 1997 there were 17 specializations offered. Students can study for two years in industrial technology, agriculture, marine technology, or forestry. Those continuing to the university can specialize in scientific, chemical, biological, or social fields. And teachers can enroll in a special program with the last year of the preparatoria devoted to the study of education.

One group of media superior schools is the *Colegio de Bachilleres,* consisting of 516 schools. The colegio has its main campus in Mexico City and branches in 20 other states.[8]

In Mexico, there are no general education requirements at the university level. Students attend the primaria for six years, the secundaria for three years, and a media superior school for three years. When they enter the university, they immediately take courses in their chosen profession.

Besides controlling the curriculum of the public schools, the SEP and the state governments also supervise private schools. The inspector for the district is responsible for ensuring that the private school conforms to the rules established by the SEP and the state government. Private schools can receive permission to modify their curriculum. For example, there are American schools, French schools, and Japanese schools in Mexico City.

In the 1992-93 school year, 91% of the students at the primary level attended public schools and 9% attended private schools. At the secondary school level, 88% of the students attended public schools and 12% attended private schools.[9]

The Organization of the Secretaría de Educación Pública

Article 3 of the Mexican constitution provides that primary and secondary education be secular, all education given by the state shall be free, and all instruction given in private institutions shall be supervised by the state. The Secretaría de Educación Pública (SEP) has the responsibility for upholding these education provisions.

The Secretarío de Educación Pública is the leader of the SEP and receives assistance from six subsecretaries. It is noteworthy that the secretaries of education have degrees in fields other than education, and most went abroad to earn their graduate degrees. (The current secretary studied biological sciences, earned his master's degree and doctorate in Mexico, and did postgraduate work at an institute dealing with cancer and immunology in Villajut, France.)

The Subsecretary of Educational Coordination is responsible for developing the programs, budget, and evaluation systems and for dealing with the computer center. In this area is the Department of International Relations, which has an extensive worldwide program. This department works with UNESCO, the Organization of American States (OAS), and various countries.

The Subsecretary of Basic and Normal Education is in charge of preschools, primary schools, special education, and education for indigenous people. When the position of Subsecretary of Middle Education was eliminated, the secondary schools, technical schools, media superior schools, training for physical education teachers, and teacher training became the responsibility of the Subsecretary of Basic Education.

The Subsecretary of Superior Education and Scientific Investigation focuses on the Universidad Pedagógica Nacional, scientific investigation, and requirements for the professions. The Subsecretary of Technological Investigation supervises agricultural schools, industrial education, technological institutes, and the Polytechnical University. Finally, the unit of information, rights of authors, and decentralization are under the Subsecretary of Planning and Coordination. The Oficialia Mayor is responsible for labor relations and the gathering of statistical information.

The council on culture and the arts, the National Institute on Anthropology and History, the *Belles Artes*, radio education, and the National Commission on Sports are decentralized units and report directly to the Secretario de Educación Pública.

To ensure that the various areas do not overlap, four councils coordinate the education activities. The Consejo Nacional Tecnico de la Educación (The National Council on Education, or CONALTE) is the most important and controls the entire system. Other councils advise on contents and methods, normal school education, and technological education.[10] In the Educational Development Plan for 2001-06 there are proposals to create a national institute for the evaluation of education, to develop a coordination effort for media superior education, and to create a plan to increase the number of students in media superior education. (This plan is on the SEP website.)

From the start of the schools movement in 1921 until 1992, the federal government was in charge of most of the schools. There were few state schools and even fewer private schools. The curriculum mandated that all teachers would be teaching approximately the same thing at the same time. In 1972 the widespread discontent among teachers and administrators resulted in a major revision of the entire curriculum. Changes focused on the normal school program, the system for teaching language, and other subjects and programs. There were minor changes in 1981 and in 1988.

Since 1989 there have been historic changes in Mexico. Dr. Carlos Salinas de Gotari, a Harvard graduate in economics, became the president in 1989. His goal was to modernize Mexico. He sold most of the state-owned businesses and increased foreign investments in Mexico by reducing the interest rate and stabilizing the peso. In addition, he changed the role of the unions. Before Salinas' presidency, *Caciques,* or labor bosses, were responsible for controlling workers and, in return for this service, they received special privileges from the government. When Salinas first became president, he ordered the arrest of Joaquín Hernández Galicia, the leader of the oil workers union. The army moved in and guarded oil facilities before the arrest. This action empowered workers, and in 1989 the teachers demanded the removal of their labor boss, Jonguitud Barrios. Directors of the schools led their teachers in huge marches, the largest numbering 250,000 people; and strikes forced Jonguitud Barrios to resign his 17-year rule of the teacher's union (SNTE). However, the strikes continued from 1989 until 1992, primarily because of an economic crisis.

In January 1992 Salinas enacted a new plan for education; and Dr. Ernesto Zedillo Ponce de León, a 40-year-old Yale-educated economist, replaced the 52-year-old Díaz Barlett as the minister of education. In order to implement the new education program, the government enacted the Acuerdo National in September 1992.[11] The acuerdo had several parts. The first was the reorganization of the school system. Each state took over the administrative functions formerly performed by the SEP. In essence, schools in each of the states became state schools while those in Mexico City remained federal schools. Thus each state also became responsible for developing material to teach the history, geography, customs, and traditions of that state, as well as for the operation and maintenance of the schools. In addition, the acuerdo lengthened the school year to 200 days.

The second part of the acuerdo focused on curriculum. For the primary school, the new emphasis was on cursive writing, critical thinking, and task-based instruction. There was less emphasis on the structural linguistic approach, and teachers were free to choose their method for initial reading instruction. The curriculum also emphasized history, geography, and civics. In math, the emphasis was on logic, algebra, and geometry. In the secondary school program, emphasis was on teaching by subject. For example, courses in biology, chemistry, and physics replaced general science in the new curriculum.

Teachers in the primary schools also have a greater say in the methods they use and, in exchange, the government requires additional education and training for teachers. On paper, it looked as though the colonial control of the past had been cast off and the modern era had begun. However, the textbooks still are printed by the federal government, the teacher training programs are approved by the federal government, and the Secretario de Educación Pública negotiates with each state concerning the budget it will receive for the schools that used to be under federal control. The federal government retains much of its control over the education system, and teachers still go to Mexico City to demonstrate and strike for more money.

The third part of the acuerdo was to ensure a professional wage to teachers. The average teacher's salary went from 1.5 times to 3.5 times the minimum wage. Currently, teachers at the lowest level on the salary schedule make 3.9 times the minimum wage.[12] However, while the goal was to provide a uniform education system, there remains a discrepancy between state and federal pay. All minimum pay raises are negotiated on a national level, so the pay disparity between federal and state schools will continue, even though the states manage the schools and the teachers do the same work.[13]

The budget for the Secretaría de Educación Pública is about 5% of Mexico's gross domestic product (GDP). In 1997 the total budget allotment for education was 155 billion pesos.[14] As with most systems of allocation, budgets have little meaning because, as the year progresses, there are changes in priorities and there are situations that require immediate attention. However, the percentage allocations to programs represent what the Mexican government perceives as important.

Sixty-nine percent of the budget directly allocated to schools (106 billion pesos) was for basic education that included pre-schools, primary schools, special education, secondary schools, and the telesecundaria program. The second-largest item in the budget was for universities and colleges (18%), followed by 13% for media superior schools and technical schools.[15]

Another area common to all primary school education in Mexico is the textbook program. The Comisión Nacional de Los Libros de Texto Gratuitos (National Commission on Free Textbooks) is responsible for printing the textbooks for all students in Mexico. From its beginning in February 1959, the commission encountered controversy. Protests were raised when the commission was created, and the Mexican Bar Association called it unconstitutional. President López Mateos defended the decision, and the first texts were published in 1960. Nineteen different groups of people in the country provided their opinions on textbook content. These first books stressed a different theme at each grade level — the community, the state, the country, the continent, and in the sixth grade, the world.[16]

In 1962, 300,000 parents held a demonstration because the new textbooks echoed the philosophies of Castro and Marx. An article in the October 1988 *Mexico Journal* noted, "The textbooks also received notoriety in the form of complaints from conservative parents and business organizations that say the textbooks are a form of state indoctrination that does not represent private initiative and family values."[17]

The books were rewritten in 1972. A commission wrote plans that included monthly objectives and activities, then they created textbooks and teacher's manuals for each grade. For the first time, the texts incorporated the works of famous authors.

New first-grade books were introduced again in 1980. The series included a teacher's manual, a *Libro Recortable* (readiness book), and parts I and II of the primer. Under the new plan, the school year was divided into eight units, with each unit containing four modules. Each unit included material to teach reading, mathematics, natural science, and social science. The teacher's manual also contained information on how to teach health and art.

The reforms of 1992 criticized the rationale that had been the basis of the literacy curriculum for the previous 14 years. The

Plan y Programas book stated that the official method was not working and that teachers needed to go back and use some of the old methods.[18]

Table 2 shows the textbooks used in each of the six grades of primary school.

Table 2. Textbooks used in the primaria.

First Grade	Third Grade	Fifth Grade
Language readiness	Language	Language
Language activities	Anthology	Anthology
Stories	Mathematics	Mathematics
Mathematics	History and geography	History
Mathematics readiness	Natural science	Natural science
Integrated text		World atlas
Readiness activities for the integrated text		
Second Grade	Fourth Grade	Sixth Grade
Language readiness	Anthology	Anthology
Stories	Language	Language
Mathematics	Mathematics	Mathematics
Mathematics readiness	Mexican historical atlas	History
Integrated text	Mathematics readiness	Geography
Readiness activities for the integrated text	Natural science	Natural science

Source: http://www.sep.gob.mx

One interesting aspect of the system is the emphasis the last administration placed on the textbooks. The president promised in 1997 and again in 1998 that all textbooks would be delivered before school started at the end of August. This was done through the use of the military and through private companies. Army helicopters landed in remote indigenous villages with textbooks, and naval vessels delivered books to villages accessible only by water. Coca-Cola, with arguably the most extensive distribution system in the world, delivered textbooks to isolated locations.[19] A more recent picture in the Mexican newspaper *Novedades* (22 June 2001) focused on army troops delivering textbooks in Veracruz. Thus delivering textbooks is still a function of the Mexican army.

Private companies print the textbooks for the secundaria, and they are free for students who cannot afford to buy them. Currently this program is for grades one and two of the secondary school. Some states buy the textbooks for all the secondary students with state funds. It is expected that all textbooks will be free by 2005.[20]

Under the new system of education, language and mathematics have become the essential parts of the primary school curriculum. Table 3 shows the number of hours per week devoted to each subject. In the first and second grades, the students study Spanish, mathematics, and an integrated program that covers natural science, history, geography, civics, art, and physical education.

In grades three to six, students study Spanish, mathematics, natural science, history, geography, civics, art, and physical education. About 45% of the time in grades one and two is devoted to language instruction, as compared to 30% in grades three to six.[21]

Table 3. Subjects and time spent per week in the primaria.

Subject	Grades 1-2	Grades 3-6
Spanish	9	6
Mathematics	6	5
Integrated program	3	
Natural science	--	3
History	--	1.5
Geography	--	1.5
Civics	--	1
Art	1	1
Physical education	1	1
Total	20	20

Source: *Plan y Programas*, p.14.

Though the new acuerdo focused on decentralization, the education system remains very strongly centralized. Historically, the best schools have been in the capital; and Mexico City's schools traditionally have more resources, full-time physical education teachers, special education teachers, and curriculum specialists. Special programs are more plentiful than in a small city in the countryside. However, the schools in the other parts of the country use the same methods, textbooks, and curriculum as in Mexico City.

Primary Schools in Mexico City

There are more than 1,045,000 students in the primary schools in Mexico City.[22] To administer this huge system, the city is divided into five administrative areas, called *direcciones* (directions). Four of the direcciones are for primarias, and one in the southern part of the city includes preschools, primarias, and secundarias. The four heads of the direcciones report to the Director General of Basic Education for Mexico City.

Each dirección is further divided into zones, with an inspector in charge of education for each zone. The inspector controls between six and 10 schools (both public and private) to ensure that the official curriculum and the policies of the SEP are being followed.[23] To become a zone inspector, the individual must have served for at least 10 years as a teacher and at least five years as a director of a school. The individual presents his or her credentials to a commission composed of SEP officials and union officials. The person receives a rating, and the name goes on a list. When there is an opening, the person with the highest rating becomes the next inspector.

The following four profiles describe some of the nuances of this work.

Inspectora Rosa is a small woman, perhaps in her late 40s or early 50s. Her office is on the second floor of a primary school in Mexico City. Inside the room are a desk, a large table, and bookshelves with the textbooks and teacher's manuals used in the schools. The inspectora describes her job:

There are always problems, and I have to solve them. A few years ago, parents were picketing the SEP because we canceled a sixth-grade class. There were too many first-grade students and not enough sixth-grade students. The director of the school closed the sixth-grade and created another first-grade. What could we do? Deny an education to all those first-graders? Finally, we had to find places in other schools for the sixth-graders. Now, things are better. Because of decentralization, industry is moving out of the central part of Mexico City, and our school population is decreasing. We now have enough books, chairs, and materials.

I am responsible for 11 schools — five morning schools, three afternoon schools, and three private schools. My job is to visit the schools and meet with the directors of the schools about policies of the SEP. We have some really good directors, and it is a pleasure to work with them. In my zone, there are classes with only 10 children. I think the SEP doesn't close these classes because they are afraid of the union.

I worked for 10 years as a teacher in the third grade. During my spare time, I studied at the normal superior; and I finally got a second job teaching math. During my 11th year of teaching, I went in front of a commission of SEP and union officials. I passed the interviews and was placed on a waiting list for director. Finally, I became a director of a school. Of course, I still taught in the secondary school. After two years, I was able to obtain a job as the secretary to a zone inspector, and that was when I gave up my job in the secondary school. After five years as a director, there was an opening for a zone inspector; and I went in front of the commission again. I made it, and I have been a zone inspector for about 10 years. Although I have to deal with problems created by the schools, by the SEP, and by the parents, I love my work.

The next person in the chain of command is the director of the school. To become a director, the person must have taught for at least 10 years and then submitted his or her credentials (course-work, evaluations, etc.) to a commission made up of members of the teacher's union and personnel from the SEP.[24] Applicants with the highest scores are promoted as positions become available. Directors interact with parents and the inspectors, and they provide public relations for the school. They have only administrative responsibilities during the session that they direct. Often directors teach in an elementary or secondary school for the second shift of the day. The directors of federal and state schools have slightly different responsibilities. Most rural schools have only one session, and so the timetable is different.

From January to May of 1996, the Dirección de Educación Primaria for Mexico City planned and developed a program to train the directors of elementary schools. Themes for the year-long training program included:

1. What is a director?
2. Establishing and using effectively consulting committees of teachers.
3. How to get teachers to cooperate and share ideas for common objectives.
4. Organizing and running effective meetings.
5. Modernization of teaching and learning.
6. Academic problems and solutions in the school (four parts).
7. Evaluation.

The training program has since been used for all new directors.[25]

Primary schools in Mexico City have walls and gates around them, so it is impossible to see what is happening inside. A worker is stationed at the gate, and access to the school is strictly controlled. Inside the gates is usually a courtyard where Monday morning flag ceremonies, assemblies, and physical education are conducted. Surrounding the courtyard are the classrooms, and the administrative offices usually are off to one side. In each school in Mexico City, there are two offices, one for the director and secretary of the morning session and one for the afternoon session.

Directora Blanca is seated at her desk in a room filled with teachers waiting for the morning session to begin. There was no school the day before because the union had called a protest march. In Mexico, the director of the school is part of the union; and in protest marches, the teachers line up behind their director. The directora talks to one of the teachers:

> "Maestra Marta, we missed you at the march yesterday. You were the only teacher from the school who did not attend."
> "My baby was sick, directora."
> "Well I am sorry that you could not go. We must go to the patio because it is time for school to start."

The directora and the teachers proceed to the patio of the school, where the secretary has set up the microphone. Students line up by class — one row for boys and one row for girls. On Mondays there is a flag ceremony; but because it is Tuesday, only announcements are made before the students proceed to class. The secretary turns on the microphone and asks the students to put their hands on their heads. Next they are asked to put their hands on their sides. When everyone is paying attention, the directora speaks and reminds the students about keeping the campus clean. On this Tuesday there also are some announcements about the Congress of Students. The Congress of Students is a contest in which a team of students from each school competes, with the winners progressing to the finals at the offices of the dirección.

After the classes march to their rooms, the directora returns to her office. In her office is a mother whose son could not return to the school until the parent speaks with the directora. The parent first pays her respects to the directora and then reaffirms that she raised a good boy. However, she explains, because of the economic crisis, there is no one home during the day to provide guidance. In the end, the boy promises to do better; and the directora promises to let him back into school. At no time was the classroom teacher consulted. The decision of the directora is final. During the entire interview the boy focused his eyes on the ground. There was respect shown to the directora by the boy and his mother.

The directora talks with the secretary about the official reports being compiled for the *SEP*. Students selected for the Congress of Students file into her office. She quizzes the students until she is satisfied that they are ready.

Next, the directora reviews the lesson plans for the week. Every Friday each teacher submits a plan for the next week, which the directora signs after reviewing. At the end of the year, she then completes evaluation forms on each teacher.

Finally, she checks her calendar to remind herself of the next meeting with the parents association. She is ready for her meeting with the zone inspector. Of course, at 12:30, Directora Blanca then goes to her second job as a sixth-grade teacher in a nearby primary school.

Director Raul's situation is quite different from Directora Blanca's. It is difficult to be a director of a school in Mexico City. However, being a director of a rural state school involves an equally difficult set of challenges. Maestro Raul was a rural teacher for nine years and a secretary to the inspector in the large town about two hours by bus from the village. Because Maestro Raul completed only nine years of education, he could not become an inspector.

In 1966 Maestro Raul talked the *ejido* (a communal farm set up by the government) into giving him land to build a school, and he talked the state into funding it. There were 50 students per class in 1966. In 1976 a federal school also was built in the town. About half of the school-aged population entered the new school. When I visited the town in 1978, the teachers were very young and still taking classes. People in the town felt that the state school was not very good. When I returned in 1989, the people in town had tremendous praise for the school and for the teachers.

Director Raul has been in charge of the rural school for 23 years. According to Raul, his school is better than the federal school because all of the teachers live in the town, while only one teacher from the federal school lives in the town.

30

For Director Raul, the school has been a series of problems. In 1984 a hurricane almost destroyed the school. The administrators and parents had to petition the state to fix it. In 1988 another hurricane did more damage. Director Raul will go to the state capital with a petition to get some more money to paint the school, but there is not much hope because of the economic crisis.

Teachers in Raul's school receive less pay and a smaller Christmas bonus than do federal school teachers, but they follow the same teaching program as their higher-paid colleagues.

In 1989 this school had 10 teachers and 305 students. The federal school had 280 students. Parents paid 150 pesos per family (US$16.50) for the year. If a family does not have the money, parents can work at the school to pay the fee.

Director Raul is proud of his accomplishments, as are the people in the town. However, he is ready to retire from the bureaucratic struggle.

Juanita, a secretary in a Mexico City primary school, has been an educator for about nine years. Six of those years have been in this school. A secretary who assists the director must be a credentialed teacher. The secretary acts as the assistant director, the nurse, the administrative clerk, and the receptionist of the school.

For six years Juanita taught in the first, second, third, or fourth grades. Three years ago the new director chose her as the secretary. Her day starts when she prepares for the opening ceremony. She takes out the microphone and assembles it so that the director can speak to the students. Her next chore is to be sure that all the teachers have signed in. This information is used to prepare a report for the SEP. The reports are typed on a computer linked to the SEP. Her other duties include making sure that teachers have enough supplies, acting as the school nurse, handling discipline problems, typing things for the director, and taking over when the director is not present. Some schools have *adjuntos* (specialist teachers) who do special tasks for the director. In other schools, the secretary handles all the work.

The Secretaría de Educación Pública is responsible for formal and cultural education in Mexico for children from birth to age 18. Preschools, primarias, secundarias, and media superior schools, as well as private schools, are supervised by the SEP. In addition, the SEP trains teachers, educates adults, provides plans and programs, and coordinates the entire system. Cultural activities are provided to the entire population. This entails a tremendous bureaucracy. The states are responsible for the buildings and the administration of the schools.

Notes

1. Allan Riding, *Distant Neighbors* (New York: Random House, 1984), p. 85.
2. *Informe de Labores, 1997-98* (Mexico: Secretaría de Educación Pública, July 1998), p. 223.
3. Ibid.
4. Ibid., p. 351.
5. Ibid., p. 219.
6. Ibid.
7. Ibid., p. 261.
8. Ibid.
9. "Las Escuelas Particulares en la Educación," *Educación 2001* (February 1996): 34.
10. Because the SEP is in a state of constant change, updated information can be found on the SEP's website: http://www.sep.gob.mx.
11. "Acuerdo Nacional para la Modernización de la Educación Básica." *Secretaría de Educación Pública* (18 May 1992).
12. *Informe de Labores,* p. 71.
13. Interview with Profra. Blanca Margarita Fuentes, SNTE, in Mexico City, 22 October 1998.
14. "Perfil de la Educación en Mexico Financiamiento de la Educación" (http://www.sep.gob.mx), p. 3.
15. Ibid.
16. Robert Miller, "Public Primary School Education in Mexico: A Focus on Reading Instruction in Mexico City," doctoral dissertation, University of San Francisco, 1980, pp. 64-65.

17. "The Textbook Controversy," *Mexico Journal*, 3 October 1988, p. 19.

18. *Plan y Programas de Estudio* (Mexico: Secretaría de Educación Pública, 1993), pp. 9-13.

19. Interview with Prof. Rafael Miranda of the Comisión Nacional de Los Libros de Texto Gratuitos, Mexico City, 15 October 1998.

20. Ibid.

21. *Plan y Programas,* p. 14.

22. *Informe de Labores*, p. 243.

23. Interviews with Dr. Francisco Silva Campachano and Sara Trejo Romero, zone officials in Mexico City, in February and March 1989. On 2 October 1998, I spoke with the zone inspectora who was filling in for a sick principal. Her goal was to become a chief inspector of a zone within five years. We talked about the problems that women encounter in the United States, and she felt that there would be no discrimination against her as she moved up the administrative ladder.

24. *Reglamento de Escalafón* (México: Comisión Nacional Mixta de Escalafon, 1975).

25. "Capacitación a Directores de Escuelas en el D.F.," *Educación 2001* (August 1996): 11-14.

CHAPTER TWO

BASIC LITERACY

It is 10 October 1998. I have visited 20 schools in the past three weeks. At this moment, I am sitting in my hotel room waiting to attend the first conference of the Guadalajara Chapter of the International Reading Association. My mind is whirling with images of Mexican teachers. One teacher gave each child a piece of paper with a number on it and used this to teach decimals. Several students stood in front of the room to show decimal places. In another class, the students cut and glued an apple in their notebooks as part of a lesson on adjectives. A third-grade teacher was on his way to the bathroom when the director and I walked into the class. He finished his task, came back, and worked in groups with the seven students on a lesson provided by the Human Rights Commission. A director of one school was late for my appointment because he had been attending a ceremony to receive an award for 50 years of distinguished service. Another director was so proud of his school that he took me to every class-room and introduced me to the teachers. He then escorted me three blocks from the school and introduced me to the inspector.

At another school, the zone inspector, the director of the school, a representative of the ministry of education, and I all descended on one poor teacher's classroom. She had a calm exterior, but I could tell she was nervous. In many classrooms, the teacher handed me the notebooks of the students and then beamed with pride as I reviewed them.

History of the Literacy Curriculum

Before discussing the current curriculum, it is desirable to examine the characteristics of the language and the practices of the past.

The relationship between reading and writing in Spanish determines some priorities in the curriculum. Spanish possesses one of the highest correlations between the spoken sound and the written symbol. There are 29 letters and 24 spoken units. The implications of this regular grapheme-phoneme relationship are important. It probably is one reason that little time is spent on teaching spelling, and also why the vocabulary and content of the textbooks are not controlled by a graded word list as are those found in basal readers in the United States.

The first nationwide textbooks were developed in the 1960s, and they led to the first standardized national curriculum. In the official curriculum, reading is an integral part of language study. Modiano, a U.S. researcher who later worked for the Instituto Nacional Indigena, summarized the program used before 1972:

> The federal and state language curriculum is outlined in the federal textbooks, workbooks, and instructional manuals. The first year of school included an introduction to reading, primarily phonic in approach, beginning with the mastery of vowel sounds, then consonants, blends, the order of presentation from easiest to most difficult. By the end of the first year, students know the entire alphabet and should be able to read by sounding out words. They also should be able to form all letters in cursive script, to know the use of capitals and small letters, also punctuation marks such as periods, question marks, and exclamation points and to understand some simple grammatical rules dealing with gender and other suffix changes.
>
> In the second year, the focus is on silent reading, reading comprehension, and the interpretation of written material. Handwriting should improve, the student should take simple dictation, free composition starts, there is a review of previous work, and they study more grammatical rules. There is a review of the semi-irregular letters in Spanish orthography, accents, and more punctuation marks.[1]

In 1972 there was a revision of the entire curriculum. Commissions developed new plan books, teacher's manuals, and textbooks. The plan books written for each of the six grades (*Plan y Programas de Estudio para la Educación Primaria)* contained objectives and activities for each month of the school year. The objectives and activities were referenced to pages in the textbooks, teacher's manuals, and student workbooks. For physical education and arts and crafts, there were descriptions of the activities to be accomplished. The teacher's books detailed the exact procedures and justified the reasons for using the procedures. Textbooks became the property of the students and were provided without cost to students in both public and private schools.

Mexican educators used a system called *método global de análisis estructural* (global method with structural analysis) that combined the global system, structural analysis, and continuous associations, including speaking, writing, and reading the same words. In the 1980-81 school year a new integrated textbook was introduced in first grade, and the following year the same system was introduced in second grade.

Under this system, first-graders received a *libro recortable* (reading readiness book). The two parts of the first-grade book were divided into eight units that corresponded to the months of the school year. Each unit contained four modules for weekly use. Within each unit were materials for teaching reading, mathematics, natural science, social science, art, and health education. The themes of the units and modules started with the study of the individual and ended with Mexico and its relationship to other countries.

The rationale for this new system was that learning increased by integrating the concepts in the curriculum. Its authors felt that it was interdisciplinary and in tune with the global methods and that it had its root in the teachings of Claparede, Decroly, and Piaget. According to the teacher's manual, students between six and eight years old see the world from a global perspective; they have difficulty with perception and observation of details. Thus a global approach would make it easier for students to handle the curriculum. In addition, the scientific method would work for various disciplines. Finally, the program taught skills sequentially, reduced the time for learning, and reinforced the retention of important concepts.

In the first grade, the method contained four parts, with the basics of reading taught in eight units. Unit 1 consisted of conversation. The teacher wrote the sight words on the board (colors, parts of the body, drinks, fruits, common animals). Students then repeated the words, identified the meaning of the words, and copied the words in their notebooks. Unit 2 used the same elements, but now the students read the words. In units 3 to 6, students identified syllables, learned consonants and vowels, and learned to write words. The students learned to write words as the teacher dictated them in units 7 and 8. Evaluation was a continuing process through all the units.

The second-grade language arts program focused on developing comprehension, eliminating confusion caused by certain letters, identifying letters, and learning difficult sound combinations. Cursive writing was not part of the curriculum.[2]

During the spring of the 1988-89 school year, the schools closed for a day. Parents, community members, teachers, students, and interested parties submitted suggestions on how to improve the schools. Officials from the SEP reviewed the suggestions and incorporated many of them into the new curriculum that was introduced during the 1993-94 school year. The curriculum that had been used since 1972 was completely revised. For the primary school, the new emphasis was on cursive writing, critical thinking, and task-based instruction. There was less emphasis on the structural linguistic approach, and teachers were free to choose their method for initial reading instruction. The emphasis was on history, geography, and civics. Math focused on logic, algebra, and geometry. Teachers in the primary schools obtained a greater say in the methods they used; thus more education and training of teachers was required.

Five major premises are the focus of the new literacy curriculum. The first is the integration of content and activities. Students learn by doing. The second is the freedom of teachers to select methods and techniques. Teachers use a combination of techniques. This is different from the previous 20 years because the "método global de analisis estructural" had been the only official method for teaching literacy. The third aspect is to honor the experiences that the students bring to the classroom. Teachers must recognize the strengths of the students. The fourth aspect is to integrate the literacy competencies into all the school activities. Finally, group work should be used.[3]

As we move into the 21st century, Mexican schools still are using the new literacy curriculum. Refinements are made as the books and the plans and programs are reviewed. How does all this work in the average classroom? The next section focuses on answering that question.

Literacy Instruction

Mexican educators consider literacy instruction to be a two-year process. Usually, the same teacher will have the students for the first two years of the primary school. Another aspect of literacy instruction is that more students are entering the primary school with preschool instruction. This leads to less time being spent on readiness.

Formal literacy instruction is divided into four parts: spoken language, written language, recreational reading, and reflections on language. According to the teacher's manual, insufficient attention was paid in the past to the development of oral activities. In the first and second grades, the students practice dialogues, narration, and description. These should be done with fluidity and correct diction. In third grade, exposition, argumentation, and debate are introduced.

In the first and second grades, the students write appropriate words and read messages, letters, and other basic forms of communication. Dictation is important in grades three to six. Writing a résumé, bibliography, and exposition in themes is taught. Students learn self-correction, analysis of texts, transmitting instructions, writing form, and personal letters. The organization of books, how to identify principal ideas, and the use of dictionaries, encyclopedias, and other systems of information are taught. In addition, students learn about diaries and newspapers.

In grades one and two, recreational reading takes the form of reading aloud by adults. The adults read stories and poetry, and the students do dramatizations. In the upper grades, students read and study the author's arguments, characterizations, and expressions; and they discuss literature in terms of the merits of the various works. The SEP prints books for the classroom libraries; and in one school that I visited, the administration holds classes to help the parents read the books to their children. In another school, the teachers held a fair for the parents and presented workshops on how parents could help teach reading to their children.

The SEP has a catalogue with more than 350 titles, and parents are encouraged to read these books to their children. There also is the realization that family issues affect the schools, so the schools distribute to parents four books, written for adults, on the topics of addiction, keeping the family healthy, sexuality, and violence.

Another aspect is reflection on the language, including basic grammar and linguistic concepts. In the first and second grades, students learn gender and number and how to communicate clearly. In the upper grades, they learn syntax, conventions of the language, and some indigenous words.

As part of the new model, teachers are free to pick the method and strategies that work best for them. In the past, teachers also used methods other than the official one; but the new policy recognizes and approves this practice.

In the questionnaire given to teachers in September and October 1998, 28 first-grade teachers responded with the methods that they used. The government encourages teachers to pick and choose from the different methods, and so many responded that they use more than one method. About 11% of the teachers indicated that they used the *onomatopeyico* system. The goal of this method is the systematic development of constant auditory associations for letters and sounds based on something or someone in the pupil's environment. For example, the vowel sound of "i" is taught in connection with the squeal of a mouse. After the student learns the sounds, syllables are taught. The word "papa" would be taught as /p/ /a/ /p/ /a/= papa. Also, they would teach *pa pe pi po pu*.[4]

About 25% of the teachers used the global method described above. Another global method is the Minjares method developed by Julio Minjares, a doctor of pedagogy at the normal superior. This is a sight-word method, and the goal is to teach students basic words and to associate these words with their meanings. Activities are used to help the students learn the words.[5] About 18% of the teachers used this method.

Thirty-two percent of the teachers used an eclectic method, borrowing from the other methods. Finally, 11% used other methods. One such method is PALEM (*Propuesta para el Aprendizaje de la Lingua Escrita y las Mathematicas*). The students learn reading comprehension through writing. The idea is to increase comprehension by having the students write about what they learn.

Jennifer Lira Mandujano analyzed four methods of reading instruction.[6] Twenty first-grade classrooms in Mexico City were selected based on the method the teacher used to teach reading. Of the four methods in the experiment — Minjares, interconductal, PALEM, and onomatopeyico — Minjares showed the greatest gains in the final reading comprehension exam. The other three, in the order listed above, followed this one. The least effective method was the onomatopeyico method. Years of service of the teachers, experience with teaching first grade, and experience with the method were not controlled in this study.

Enrique Farfán Mejia and Pilar Amador Alvarez studied classes in the outskirts of Mexico City to determine the effectiveness of the Minjares, onomatopeyico, interconductal, and PALEM methods.[7] The study focused on reading letters, syllables, and words and phrases; visual and auditory discrimination; and knowing the child through writing, which is the basis for evaluating PALEM and comprehension. The investigators developed a 10-question test to measure comprehension. The results showed that the interconductal method, which stresses critical thinking, was the best for reading comprehension, followed by Minjares, PALEM, and onomatopeyico. Of course, the matter is not settled; and there will be more studies to determine the "best" method of teaching reading.

The Secretaría de Educación Pública has simplified planning for instruction in Mexico. Each student and teacher receives free textbooks for their grade. In the first grade, they use the *Ficheros* (which is a teacher reference book filled with class activities), a book of stories, a reading readiness book, an activity book for language, a reading readiness book for math, and a math book. While each teacher is free to use any method or strategy of instruction that he or she deems proper, including materials produced by commercial publishers, all of the tasks that the students are expected to be able to do are outlined in the *Avance Programáticos,* and pages in the student material are referenced to these tasks. Most teachers use this book because it is organized for instruction. In the first-grade edition of the *Avance Programáticos*, the day is divided into three blocks. The first is for language, the second for mathematics, and the third is the integrated program. The teacher should average nine hours per week for language study, six hours for mathematics, and three for the integrated program (natural science, history, geography, and civics). There is one hour for art and one hour for physical education.

Block one is for the first two months of school. After considering the abilities of the students, the teacher chooses the tasks from the *Avance Programático*.[8] Each task is linked to all or one of four books. For example, if the task is for the teacher to read stories to the students, the teacher looks in the *Avance Programáticos* under "Reading Book" to see a list of the stories. In addition, there is a group activity listed in the *Ficheros* column. Another example is analysis of sounds. The teacher finds the pages listed in the column under "Readiness Book" (these are to be cut out) and then finds the pages in the column under "Activity Book" where these items will be pasted.

Block one for math and block one in the integrated program also reinforce language skills and focus on vocabulary building. Readiness skills are developed in math, where students learn to make comparisons, to organize materials into tables, and to classify items. The integrated program focuses on body parts, health, the senses, and civic activities using listening, speaking, and art. After the teacher picks the activities for the language, math, and integrated blocks, a weekly lesson plan is submitted to the principal for approval. All teachers in all grades submit their plans.

Every September the directors of the schools receive the results of the sixth-grade tests. The zone results are reported in math (logic and resolution of problems) and language (reading, comprehension, and grammar). Data are provided for a five-year period. The director and the teachers meet to review the results together. This report is called the *Indicadores de Culidad*. There is a second exam at the end of the secundaria.

Profile of a Teacher

The following composite profile of a Mexican teacher will put this literacy information in perspective. In Mexico, teachers are not called by their last names. It is maestro or maestra (teacher) and then their first name.

In October, Maestra Queta had a six-pound baby boy. This was an exciting moment in her life. The administration found a substitute teacher for her classes, so she took six weeks off, knowing that her students would not have to stay home during her absence. After she returned to the classroom, she described her teaching routine:

> Life is very difficult for me. I don't want to leave my baby in the morning, but I must work. I get up about six a.m. and arrive at my school at eight a.m. This year, I'm teaching first grade. In the past, I've taught first and second grades.
>
> It's Monday morning at 7:45 a.m. The gates of the school are open, and students come to the main plaza area. They're in uniform, and they line up by class. I report to the office and sign in. Next, I stand in front the class. At eight a.m. there's a flag raising ceremony, and my students march to class. On the other days of the week, the students line up and then report to the classroom. I take roll, and the day's activities begin. The activities center on language instruction and

mathematics. There's endless cutting and pasting from the *Libro Reecortable*. This is done as a prereading activity. The students line up at the desk to have their work checked.

When I introduce a new activity related to reading, writing, or math, the material is written on the board, and the students copy the information in their notebooks. After they finish copying, one or two students go to the board and write the correct answer. Everyone in the class claps. The students then copy this information in their notebooks. I either have the students come up to the desk, or I go around to each desk and check the work in the notebooks. This activity continues for 20 minutes to an hour.

Another activity begins. The students use their books occasionally, but mostly they use the notebooks. Break is from 10:00 to 10:30, and the students can buy food. Poor students receive a free breakfast [milk and bread]. After the break, they study for another two hours. In my class we will study mathematics. Two days a week we have P.E., and one day a week we do art projects. At 12:30, the students go home. This program continues for the 200 days of the school year.

I sign out and I go to a second school and repeat the process. Afternoon sessions start at 2 p.m. and end at 6:30 p.m. I can hardly wait for school to end so that I can go and see my baby. Life is very difficult for me because I work from 8 a.m. to 6:30 and I travel on the metro for another 45 minutes each way. I am forced to work two shifts because I can't live on one salary. Everything is so expensive. I teach to help the children of my country.

There are other activities in the schools. All students will have a minimum of one hour of physical education per week. Throughout the year, there will be special programs to honor various events, such as Independence Day.

During the first month of school, the students are evaluated by the classroom teacher using teacher-developed tests and by teacher observation of the student's abilities. The director of the school receives this information. Every two months a report card is sent home.

Changes in Mexican Education

In this chapter I have focused on some impressions of the Mexican classrooms, the literacy curriculum, methods of teaching reading, teacher planning, and the organization of a day in the life of a teacher. This information was derived from publications and from observations. To complete the discussion of literacy instruction in Mexico, I shift now to the changes in the system over the past 20 years, based on my questionnaire and classroom observation data.

During the 1978-79 school year, 300 questionnaires were returned from the teachers in the 26 schools used in the study. In the 1988-89 follow-up study of 11 schools, 104 questionnaires were returned; and in the final study during the 1998-99 school year, 228 questionnaires were returned.

In 1978-79, 52% of the classrooms contained more than 40 students. That percentage was reduced to 6.3% in 1988-89 and zero in 1998-99. In fact, 43% of the classrooms contained 20 or fewer students in 1998-99.

The earthquake of 1985 destroyed many houses, and in many areas of the city housing is being converted to commercial uses. These factors have increased the cost of housing, and people have moved away from the city center. Thus classes are extremely small. Afternoon schools, which run from 2:00 until 6:30, generally contain fewer students than morning schools. It is not unusual to find fewer than 10 students in a class in an afternoon school.

In terms of chairs, desks, books, and other materials, 91% of the teachers had enough chairs and desks and 86% had enough books, but only 63% had enough other materials. However, in many schools the desks were in need of replacement. In one school, the principal was holding a special program on Saturday for parents to help repair the school's furniture. He expected about 20 parents to help.

The passing rate has improved dramatically. In 1978-79, 24.2% of the teachers reported that they passed between 81% and 100% of the boys. For girls, 27.7% of teachers reported this rate.

In 1998-99, 95% of the teachers reported that they passed between 81% and 100% of the boys. For girls, 97% of teachers reported this rate. Concerning the students in their classrooms, about 50% of the teachers felt that from 61% to 80% of the students were prepared for the class, and another 18% felt that 81% to 100% were prepared. The goal to have more students pass to the next grade has been met.

Now the problem is to provide adequate education so that the students are *prepared* for the next grade. In 1970 almost 65% of the students dropped out before completing the sixth grade. That percentage is now down to 15%. The task of improving the quality of instruction may be easier in Mexico City because most of the students in the sample schools spoke Spanish. In the 228 responses to the questionnaires, only two teachers indicated that they taught a student who spoke an indigenous language.

On Friday, 12 October 2001, an article in the *News* reported that 16,000 indigenous children living in Mexico City are not allowed to attend school because they lack birth certificates. One legislator's plan is to establish 31 care centers for these children. Each center would have an average capacity of 60 children, and the centers would meet the physical and the educational needs of this group.[9]

When asked about the official guides, all teachers now use them, compared with 94.8% during the 1988-89 year and 98% during 1978-79. Practically all teachers modify the program and use materials not contained in the *Avance Programáticos.* Most teachers give homework, and 78% of the teachers indicated that they give more than three hours of homework each week. Many teachers use commercially prepared materials.

The teachers indicated that the students faced a series of social problems. The most frequently mentioned was divorce. Others included little guidance from the family because both parents worked and lack of food. In some areas of Mexico City, students sniff glue to cope with hunger.

Teachers also were asked to rate their schools and the Mexican education system. Sixty-four percent rated their schools as good or excellent, and 38% rated the system as good or excellent. First-grade teachers were asked about preschool, and only 41% stated that 81% to 100% of their students had attended the preschool program. During the 1978-79 school year, when cursive writing was not part of the curriculum, 31% of the teachers taught cursive writing in their classrooms. Now, even though cursive writing is part of the curriculum, only 49% of the teachers work with cursive writing.

The next section of the questionnaires addressed classroom practices. In the 1998-99 questionnaires, 81% of the teachers reported that they focus on reading readiness, 90% on vocabulary, 88% on comprehension, 87% on oral reading, 74% on memorization, and 91% on teaching grammar. Concerning classroom techniques and materials, 90% have class discussions, 87% use classroom libraries, 86% use small-group instruction, and 86% read to the students. It is interesting that the teaching of readiness was reported significantly less often on the 1998-99 questionnaire than in 1978-79 and 1988-89. This may be a result of the increased number of students attending preschool. The use of memorization also was down, with only 74% of the respondents requiring the activity. Except for memorization, 80% to 100% of the teachers have used all of the strategies and materials listed over the last 20 years.

More than 80% of the teachers have access to television and movies in the school. Only 43% have a photocopier, and only 22% have access to a fax machine. There was a computer in each of the schools observed, but only 27% of the teachers have access to a computer. The computer in the school is used for administrative functions, and there is a direct link to the Secretaría de Educación Pública.

Classroom observations were made in each target year: 1978-79, 1988-89, and 1998-99. The observations lasted from 20 minutes to 90 minutes per class. Each interaction in the classroom was recorded, and the items were coded and grouped into five areas: routine, discipline, oral, written, and activities.

The main, consistent activity during all three observations was students lining up at the teacher's desk to have their work corrected. In 1978-79, discipline consisted of exercises to get the students' attention because the classes were so large that year. In 1978-79 and 1998-99, teachers praised students more than they criticized them.

Reading aloud and recitation dominated oral work in 1978-79. This changed in 1988-89 and 1998-99, when teachers querying their students became the main activity. Recitation was still important, but it occurred less often than in 1978-79.

During the 20-year period of this investigation, the most prevalent model was the teacher writing on the blackboard and the students copying the material into their notebooks. Next, the students would go up to the board and fill in the answers. The students would check their work, and the teacher would check to see that it was done correctly. During the 1988-89 and 1998-99 school years, more students worked on their own and more students wrote paragraphs instead of words or sentences.

The most important instructional technique during the 20-year period was for the students to make things. During the 1978-79 year, students made puppets, maps, and cubes. They cut out and pasted things in their notebooks. During the 1998-99 school year, teachers played games with small groups of students and made posters to visualize concepts, and the students used cutouts to learn math skills. One class wrote recipes and read them to the class. Photocopied handouts were used in both 1988-89 and 1998-99; however, this practice was not widespread.

Each school has the traditional standardized curriculum but, at the same time, each is unique. For example, the teachers and students at Sara Manzano have colored smocks, and everyone wears them. This leads to cohesion among the staff and the students. At this school, the physical education instructors teach folk dancing, and all of the students participate. At Estado de Hidalgo, there is a swimming pool where all students learn how to swim. At Republic de Panama, they have an experimental computer lab, and every student is able to use the computers twice a month. At Luis Murillo, the students made a record. Chirpre is a *turno completo* school, where the students study the normal curriculum from 8:00 a.m. to 12:30 p.m. and then return from 2:00 p.m. until 5:00 p.m. for crafts, dance instruction, and music. The number of these *turno completo* schools is growing each year. The current Secretary of Education wants all schools to be this type of school by 2006.

The Mexican system of education within population centers is dynamic and changing to meet the needs of the students. As with all systems of education, there are strengths and weaknesses. Even though the system is centralized, it cannot be viewed as monolithic.

At the SEP level, major changes are announced every six years. The system at the school level is more stable, and change tends to be gradual — as illustrated by the *método global*, the approved system used to teach reading, which lasted from 1972 to 1993. Also, the concept of an integrated approach to teaching in the first and second grades lasted for more than 10 years.

From interviews with teachers and directors, the most important changes in the past 20 years have been improvements in the quality of the textbooks and the curriculum, the freedom allowed teachers in the *Avance Programáticos*, and parent involvement in the schools. I have been in front of schools on parent meeting days, and there have been from 50 to 100 parents waiting to attend the parent meeting. Also, teachers are providing a wider range of activities in the classroom, and they are more involved with the students.

Teachers feel good about their schools, as shown by the approval ratings in the questionnaires. More teachers are decorating their classrooms, and student work is being exhibited on the walls in the classroom.

The data for the 1998-99 school year indicate that more teachers are asking their students questions. However, observations indicated that most questions require literal or factual answers, rather than answers that employ critical thinking skills. During most classroom observations, I did not hear many "why" questions.

Instruction is provided to the whole group. It seemed that the brightest students had to sit and wait for the rest of the class to catch up. The students who were having trouble or had mild forms of ADHD would move between chairs or not remain on task. Students with severe problems received remedial instruction, which will be discussed later.

Mexico has moved from a very rigid system of teaching literacy to one that is highly flexible. However, all teachers are accountable for teaching the required skills, and there is standardization because all teachers and students use the same textbooks.

Notes

1. Nancy Modiano, "Reading Comprehension in the National Language: A Comparative Study of Bilingual and All Spanish Approaches to Reading Instruction in Selected Indian Schools in the Highlands of Chiapas, Mexico," doctoral dissertation, New York University, 1966.
2. *Libro Para el Maestro* (Mexico: Secretaría de Educación Pública, 1981).
3. *Educación Basica, Primaria, Plan y Programas de Estudio* (Mexico: Secretaría de Educación Pública, 1993), pp. 23-24.
4. Eleanor Thonis, *Literacy for America's Spanish Speaking Children* (Newark, N.J.: International Reading Association, 1976), pp. 28-32.
5. Julio Minjares Hernandez, "El Método Minjares," in *La Enseñanza de la Lectura por Medio de los Métodos Globales* (Mexico: Editorial Pax, 1989), pp. 17-26.
6. Jennifer Lira, "Aprender a Leer," *Educación 2001* (January 1999): 28-31.
7. Enrique Farfán Mejia and Pilar Amador Alvarez, "La Enseñanza de la Lecto-Escritura,"*Educación 2001* (February 1998): 25-28.
8. Secretaría de Educación Pública, *Avance Programático* (Mexico: Secretaría de Educación Pública, 1993).
9. "16,000 Indigenous Children Kept Out of School for Lacking a Birth Certificate," *The News*, Mexico City, 12 October 2001. http://the newsmexico.com

CHAPTER THREE

RURAL AND BILINGUAL SCHOOLS AND ADULT EDUCATION

Of the 84 million people in Mexico in 1996, 23 million lived in rural areas.[1] During a teacher's strike in May 1997, teachers from the poorest regions in Mexico told of teachers and students who must walk through rough terrain for hours to get to school. Four walls with no roof and a dirt floor passes for a school building, and many teachers said that they must buy school supplies from their salaries.[2]

The model for rural schools in Mexico is one of small schools scattered throughout the countryside, rather than large schools serving several communities, which has become the norm in the United States. Mexican rural schools remain because the people do not have adequate transportation and the roads often are impassable during storms. The schools are built so that the children can walk to them. However, there arc not enough schools to meet the needs of all students. In Mexico there are some 200,000 localities, and 75% have fewer than 100 inhabitants.[3]

The government recognizes the socioeconomic problems associated with rural poverty and has several compensatory programs. The first program is PARE (Programa para Abatar el Rezago Educativo), which serves regular primary rural and indigenous schools in the states of Chiapas, Guerrero, Hidalgo, and Oaxaca. This program began in 1991-92. PAREB (Programa para Abatar el Rezago en Educación Basica) started in 1994-95 and serves primary and secondary schools in the states of Campeche, Durango, Guanajuato, Jalisco, Michoacán, Puebla, San Luis Potosí, Tabasco, Veracruz, and Yucatán. PIARE (Programa Integral para Abitir el Rezago Educativo) began in 1995 and serves initial education, preschool, primary schools, and adult education. The program serves regular primary school education, rural schools, and indigenous schools in the states of Chihuahua, Coahuila, Lima, México, Nayarit, Querétaro, Quintana Roo, Sinaloa, Sonora, and Zacatecas and serves beginning education in 22 states. This program also provides education to smaller communities in 23 states. The next program is PRODEI (Programa para el Desarrollo de la Educación Inicial). This program, started in 1991, focuses on children under four years old. The program operates in the states of Chiapas, Guanajuato, Guerrero, Hidalgo, México, Michoacán, Oaxaca, Puebla, San Luis Potosí, and Yucatán. Finally, the PQED (Programa de Apoyo a Escuelas en Desventaja), which started in 1992, operates 100 schools for the disadvantaged. These schools are in states where PARE, PAREB, and PIARE do not have operations.[4]

During the 1997-98 school year, these programs distributed more than 94,000 packets developed for students. The packets included pencils, colored pencils, crayons, erasers, notebooks, and protractors. More than 90,000 helpers, supervisors, and school directors received special training through these programs. They built 2,900 more spaces for classes, added additions to existing schools, and repaired and maintained school facilities. Parent associations also were formed; by the end of the 1997-98 year, 14,000 associations were in existance. Each association received about 5,000 pesos to buy blackboards, paint, and so forth.[5]

Approximately 150,000 communities have fewer than 100 inhabitants. The Educación Communitaria program extends education services to these people. More than 27,000 literacy workers went into 23,708 communities to teach the children.[6] As I will explain in the next section, people in these communities have other options, such as albergue escolares.

Although the government is attempting to help the poor, each program has its critics. An evaluation of PARE appeared in *Educación 2001*. The author made several criticisms of the program: 1) the program does not recognize the uniqueness of the rural schools and therefore tries to use the model of urban schools; 2) there are not enough literate people in many communities to reinforce the skills taught in the schools; 3) there is a tremendous amount of migration in these communities; and 4) most of the teachers are poor farm workers; and though they have been to school, they tend to be very provincial and authoritarian in their teaching.[7]

In a speech given at Monterey, Nuevo León, Reyes Taméz Guerra, the secretary of public education, said that only 1% of the indigenous youth and 3% of young people from rural areas study at the university level. This compares with 45% of middle-class youth and 11% of the youth from urban families of limited resources who study at the university.[8]

Bilingual Literacy Instruction

As part of the 1989 study, I boarded the evening train to Oaxaca. As I slept, the train made its winding trip south through the mountains to the state capital. My first visit was to the SEP office in Oaxaca to obtain a letter of introduction. Next, I took the bus for 10 miles over the high desert until it finally stopped on a country road. The school was about 10 miles up this road. Luckily, a pickup truck offered me a ride. I arrived at San Pablo Guila, Oaxaca, a Zapoteco village. The houses were made of adobe, and the people slept on the floor instead of on beds. All the teachers and the director were Zapotecs. Bilingual books were available, but they did not use them.

The school itself was very modern and well maintained. Physically, the school consisted of several buildings constructed on concrete slabs. Inside the director's office were new chairs and tables purchased by the parents and the SEP. The school contained 11 teachers and 308 students. Grades one and two were taught bilingually, but grades three to six were taught only in Spanish. There were 11 classes in the school, with an average of 28 students per class. They wanted a secondary school, but there was no money to build one.

The poorest people in Mexico are the indigenous people. In 1997 these included more than seven million people in 52 ethnic groups. Programs have been developed for these people, and Mexican administrations have shown a spirit of social responsibility toward the Indians because this is an essential element of the philosophy of the Mexican Revolution.[9] Most of the indigenous people live in isolated communities in the poorer states of Mexico.

From the 16th century onward, the indigenous people suffered enslavement, forced conversions to Christianity, and destruction of their populations by disease. Today, as has been the case throughout history, they are at the bottom of Mexican society. The government has tried various approaches to deal with these groups. In 1770, the extinction of Indian languages was ordered. This policy did not work. However, approximately 93 Indian languages have disappeared since the conquest.[10]

Between 1911 and 1917 a system of rural schools was developed primarily for the indigenous population. By 1931, 600,000 students attended 7,000 rural schools with 8,000 teachers. Eighty-one percent of the communities with fewer than 4,000 people did not have schools. Between 1920 and 1930, only 2% of the students continued beyond the second grade. In 1936, the Department of Indian Affairs was created, and in 1948 the Instituto Nacional Indigenista (INI) was established. INI became the agency responsible for health education and the welfare of the indigenous people. In the 1970s, the indigenous people gained the right to hold legal title to their lands (these titles had been taken away during the Díaz period of 1876-1911) and a great debate began over how best to work with the indigenous peoples. One approach was isolation with INI protection. The goal was to use INI as a buffer against the larger society. The second approach was to bring the indigenous into the mainstream by preparing them to work within the larger society. The last approach focused on the government providing essential assistance but without paternalism and manipulation. Under President Lopez Portillo (1976-1982) there was greater emphasis on bilingual education, and indigenous-language radio stations were developed.

In 1936 the Summer Institute of Linguistics, invited by President Cardenas, transcribed the indigenous languages. This was important because the indigenous languages were transcribed in the Roman alphabet. Thus the transition into Spanish was not very difficult. The members of the institute were Christian missionaries, and in 1983 they were officially evicted from Mexico. However, in practice, they still continued their work.

Indigenous people remain the most marginalized sector of Mexican society. More than 40% of those 15 years and older were illiterate in 1990 (three times the national rate), and 36% between the ages of six to 14 did not attend school.[11]

Since the 1960s, the Mexican government has realized the implication of bilingual research, which has shown that students learn faster when the native language is used as a vehicle for instruction. However, bilingual education is not easily done when there are 52 ethnic groups and more than 80 languages and dialects. For example, there are only 12 people who speak Opata, as compared to 1,197,328 who speak Náhualt.[12] This creates a tremendous problem in finding teachers who speak these languages and in developing textbooks for the various groups.

In 1978 the Dirección General de Educación Indigena (DGEI) was created as a specialized branch of the SEP and charged with developing programs to increase the literacy rate among indigenous people. The focus is on bilingual textbooks, bilingual radio programs, Centers of Social Integration, albergues escolares and escuelas albergues, and education programs directed at women.

The most ambitious project has been the development of first-language textbooks for the 52 ethnic groups and the 80 languages and dialects that these people speak. As of this writing, 47 languages and dialects are used in textbooks (see Table 4). This accounts for 70% of the students who speak indigenous languages. More than 1,100,000 books were printed during the 1997-98 school year.[13]

The series includes full-color textbooks, teacher's manuals, and specific goals and objectives for the teachers. Teaching techniques vary from book to book because native speakers of the Indian languages developed the materials and the teaching techniques.

Table 4. Indigenous languages with available textbooks (and area).

Amuzgo (Guerrero)
Chatino (Zenzontepec, Oaxaca)
Chinanteco (the Sierra, Oaxaca)
Chinanteco (Ojitlán, Oaxaca)
Chinanteco (Usila, Oaxaca)
Chol (Chiapas, Tabasco)
Chontal (Tabasco)
Cora (Nayarit)
Hñahñu (Hidalgo)
Hñohño (Querétaro)
Huichol (Durango, Jalisco, Nayarit)
Maya (Yucatán, Campeche, Quintana Roo)
Mayo (Sinaloa, Sonora)
Mazahua (México)
Mazateco (Ixacatlan, Oaxaca)
Mazateco (Huautla, Oaxaca)
Mazateco (San José Ind., Oaxaca)
Mazateco (Soyaltepec, Oaxaca)
Mixe (Guichicovi, Oaxaca)
Mixe (the middle zone, Oaxaca)
Mixteco (the mountains, Guerereo)
Mixteco (the high region, Oaxaca)
Mixteco (Jamiltepec, Oaxaca)
Náhuatl (Huasteca region, Hidalgo)
Náhuatl (north Puebla)
Náhuatl (Guerrero)
Pame (San Luis Potosí)
Popolopuca (Veracruz)
Purépecha (Michoacán)
Rarámuri (Chihuahua)
Seri (Sonora)
Tének (San Luis Potosí)
Tepehua (Hidalgo, Veracruz)
Tepehuano (Durango)
Tlapaneco (Guerrero)
Tojolabal (Chiapas)
Totonaco de Huauchinango (Puebla)
Totonaco (Veracruz)
Triqui (Chicahuastla, Oaxaca)
Tzeltal (Chiapas)
Tzotzil (Chiapas)
Yaqui (Sonora)
Zapoteco (Miahuatlán, Oaxaca)
Zapoteco (Villa Alta, Oaxaca)
Zoque (Chimalapa, Oaxaca)
Zoque (Copainalá, Chiapas)
Zoque (Ocotepec, Chiapas)

Mexican officials have stated that this system would entice local teachers to use the materials.

Within each set of books for the indigenous groups is a book without words in which students manipulate pictures and numbers to learn reading readiness skills, such as shapes, color, and direction. Next, the students are given a primer in their native language. After they finish this primer, they can read and write (at a very basic level) in their language. These skills are transferred to special primers that are modified, monolingual, Spanish primers.

The radio bilingual education program is designed to teach literacy in the native language, transmit the culture of the native group, and teach literacy in Spanish. Since most of the indigenous villages do not have electricity, they use battery-powered radios. Teachers from the indigenous areas go to INI facilities and produce radio programs in the native languages. During the day, the stations broadcast music and programs on health, education, infant care, and similar subjects. "Que Hable el Corazon?" (What Does Your Heart Say?) is the most popular program. This program focuses on the traditions of the indigenous community and uses people from various villages to read the scripts.

Another technology being used is television. In the larger villages, the government is equipping 2,000 schools with satellite dishes. The majority of the programs are in Spanish, but 90 programs have been developed around themes for indigenous people.

There also are several special types of school, including the Centros de Integración Social, the albergues escolares, and the escuelas albergues. The Centros de Integración Social, for students over 14 years old, offer training in various occupations. Agriculture is stressed. There are 32 such centers with 5,300 students in all. The albergues escolares are primary schools that are not bilingual. The students, who often are from very isolated communities, stay at the school from Monday until Friday. There are 1,250 of these schools serving 63,900 students. Escuelas albergues are bilingual schools for students aged six to 14. Again, the students stay at the school from Monday until Friday. About 50 boys and girls live in an albergue escolar or an escuela albergue. They live in a dormitory with a supervisor and two cooks. There is a school on the grounds that children from the community and the residents of the albergue attend. The school is run by the DGEI, and the dormitory is run by INI. There are 1,076 albergues in 21 states. A typical routine would be to hold classes from 8:00 a.m. to 1:00 p.m., lunch from 1:00 p.m. to 3:00 p.m., sports and chores from 3:00 p.m. to 7:00 p.m., dinner from 7:00 p.m. to 8:00 p.m., and homework from 8:00 p.m. to 9:00 p.m.[14]

The last program concerns the development and education of Indian women. This program started in 1978 and ended in 1992. Programs included literacy instruction in the native language and training in Spanish, care and handling of infants, health education, and primary school education. The woman in charge of each center had from six to nine years of schooling, was trained for three months, and then received from 15 to 30 days per year of additional training. These programs were conducted in 266 centers, and 10,335 women participated during the 1987-88 school year. There were about 20 women in each center.[15]

The Centros de Educación Initial have replaced this program, and the centers focus on families with children up to age four. There is one teacher for 25 students, and they use *promotores* (individuals teaching without a secondary school certificate) instead of teachers with 16 years of education. The students attend preschool at age four and then start the primaria at age six.

It is difficult to find primary school teachers for the Indian schools, so their training system is different from that used for regular teachers. Potential teachers go to the primaria, secundaria, and the media superior for a total of 12 years. Then they attend a special course for six months, and then are assigned a classroom. The future teachers learn sanitation and agricultural techniques, as well as academic subjects. During the weekends, summers, and vacation periods, they take courses on how to teach so that they can receive the *licenciatura* (bachelor of arts). Given the poverty of the indigenous villages, the salary is relatively high, so more men work as primary school teachers. Also, they receive 90 days of extra pay at Christmas.[16]

There are many education programs for indigenous people. INI handles the living conditions of albergues escolares, and the DGEI handles initial education, preschool, primarias, and secundarias that serve more than 100 people. INEA (adult education) provides bilingual textbooks for adults, and CONAFE provides preschool and primary school in communities where there are less than 100 people. The teachers in the CONAFE program are students fulfilling their social service requirements.

The government is committed to improving literacy among the non-Spanish-speaking population. With the help provided from bilingual textbooks, trained bilingual teachers, special schools, as well as radio and television programs, this population is learning how to read and write in Spanish, as well as in their native languages.

Adult Education

The routine actions of people often provide insight into the major problems of a society. I was on a bus heading for the coast, and we stopped outside Tepic. An older man's spouse needed to use the bathroom. It was obvious that they could not read the signs above the doors. She ended up in the men's room, and he stood guard outside. How powerless it must feel to be surrounded by the written word and not be able to understand.

Illiteracy is a problem that plagues Mexican society. It is impossible to create a modern society without addressing the education needs of the population. This realization has forced educators and government officials to try many techniques and schemes to reduce the illiteracy rate and to educate the population.

A Brief History of Literacy Campaigns and Programs. At the time of the Mexican Revolution, more than two-thirds of the Mexican population could not read or write. Besides increasing the availability of schools for school-age children, "anti-illiteracy" campaigns were inaugurated in the 1920s and 1930s. In the 1940s, a sweeping effort to have "each one teach one" produced observable results.[17] In the campaign of 1944-46, ten million *cartillas* and workbooks were printed and distributed.[18] These books were printed for adults, and the approach was primarily phonetic.

The 1970 census reported that Mexico had 6.7 million illiterates and one million more people who did not speak Spanish. In the group of 13 million adults (persons over 15 years old) that were considered literate, more than nine million had not studied beyond the fourth grade. The response to these statistics was a new program, Educación Para Todos.

Educación Para Todos was a program designed to teach literacy to 16 million people. The first phase of the program (1978-80) was to develop the system and to acquire data regarding the problem. Phase two (1980-82) was designed to improve and evaluate the program. There were six components to the program. First, there was an expansion of the special primary programs, such as providing more albergues escolares and more centers for the teaching of literacy. The second component was to expand primary education to meet national demand. *Cursos comunitarios* were offered in communities with 200 to 500 inhabitants. The teacher lived in the community and was paid 77.40 pesos per month, which came from state, federal, and private sources. Teachers in this program completed nine years of school and attended a special training course. The teacher, besides teaching literacy, was responsible for helping the people with illness, agriculture, and other types of problems. The third component of the program was to provide Spanish-language instruction for Indian children. This meant that preschools would teach the children to speak Spanish. In Huejutla, Hidalgo, for example, I attended a meeting of Spanish-language supervisors at the INI center on 30 October 1978. They used the Montessori method, and classes were limited to 20 students.

The fourth component of the program was to teach literacy to adults. This was done in Centers of Literacy in communities with more than 2,500 persons. Also, regional centers of basic education were established in 28 cities. The fifth component was to provide correspondence courses to teach literacy to adults. Also, the government planned to develop 600 radio lessons of 15 minutes duration; these would correspond to the contents of the official textbooks for grades four, five, and six. They would be made into 15-minute cassettes and then used in the classroom. The sixth and final component was to integrate literate adults into regular education programs and to develop the community by promoting cultural activities. This program was coordinated by the Consejo Nacional de Educación de Grupos Marginados. This group consisted of the Secretarío de Educación Pública, the director of the social volunteers, the secretaries of the state committees for the Educación Para Todos program, one representative from the national parents association, and the Director General de Educación de Grupos Marginados.

Materials and a trained literacy worker were provided to small groups of illiterates. In the four-month training, illiterates learned to read, write, and do basic mathematics. The literacy worker used a kit based on the techniques developed by Paulo Freire, the great Brazilian educator.[19]

The literacy method was called the *palabra generadora*, or "generative word." Sixteen words were identified that contain all the sounds of the language. These words were also important to the environment of adult illiterates. In Spanish, the concepts were shovel, piñata, vaccine, house, medicine, garbage, tortillas, milk, the market, the family, a cantina, work, guitar, education, Mexico, and a health clinic.

In the kit carried by the literacy worker were pictures of each of these objects. Each object was shown in a setting familiar to the illiterates. After the pictures were presented, there was a discussion of the picture so that the word had meaning for the illiterates. Next, the word was divided into syllables, and the vowel in each syllable was changed. For example, the word for shovel is pala. The teaching progression was:

pa la, po lo, pe la, pu lu, pi li

The students then combined the syllables and made new words. These words were discussed and written, and then the process began with the next word.

Students also studied mathematics. They were taught to write numbers up to 1,000 and learned the concepts of equality, subtraction, addition, multiplication, and division.

On 15 May 1981 a new program was announced: open education. At this time, 6.6 million Mexicans over age 15 could not read or write, and 13 million more had not finished the primary school. The new program expanded on the goals of the Educación Para Todos program by offering primary and secondary schooling for adults. By 1984, the Instituto Nacional para la Educación de los Adultos (INEA) was taking an active part in the literacy programs.

In 1989, 4.2 million people were illiterate and 20.2 million had not finished their elementary schooling. The decentralized approach was not working. The goals outlined in the education modernization program of 1989-1994 called for a more coordinated effort. The new plan called for 1) materials to be developed that are related to family life, working conditions, and social environment; 2) a special literacy program for ethnic groups; 3) radio and TV literacy programs; 4) a national system for crediting and certifying adult basic education; 5) a research network; and 6) work with corporations and industries to provide workplace education.

Literacy training also was done through television. Each person who enrolled in a television course received a workbook. The lessons on the television corresponded to the workbook lessons. Students who enrolled in a television course received periodic visits from a literacy worker. The student also could phone a toll-free number or write a letter to receive an answer to a problem or a question. In addition, the INEA developed materials for 14 indigenous groups in the following languages: Maya, Náhuatl, Otomí, Purépecha, Totonaco, Mixteco, and Zapoteco.

Statistics from INEA show that during the 1987-88 school year, 666,858 students were involved in the literacy groups. At the primary school level, 772,608 adults were involved in their programs and 203,103 adults were involved at the secondary level. About 803,300 adults were given basic education skills at their work places.[20]

Adult Education Today. In 1993 the definition of basic education was changed. Prior to this date, the definition was only six years of primary school. Now it is six years of primary school and three years of secondary school.

Significant gains have been made in basic education (primary plus secondary schooling). In 1970, 91% of the adult population (over 15 years of age) had not completed basic education. Today, that number stands at 58.6%. It should be noted that the illiteracy rate is now only 10.6% (as of 1995). But the problem still is large. Of more than six million illiterates in the nation, 1.5 are indigenous people. And, in general, more women (12.66%) than men (8.42%) are illiterate. Illiteracy rates are higher among older adults than among younger adults.

The government sponsors a welfare program called Progresa, which provides money to families on the condition that they send their children to school and to the doctor for checkups and vaccines. The program is for the poorest families in the country. Families with girls receive more money than those with boys. This is an effort to reverse the lower status accorded to daughters in many indigenous families. This has the effect of decreasing the illiteracy rates because more girls will be going to school.[21]

The INEA is involved in three areas of education: primary literacy, primaria, and secundaria. In each area there are programs that reach out to a broad range of people. INEA has offices in 33 states. It does not do the teaching but develops materials and coordinates between private companies and agencies of the government. They have specialists that train people.

About 579,000 people are enrolled in literacy (*alfabetización*) courses. The courses are conducted in 26 indigenous languages, as well as Spanish. Primaria and secundaria classes are taught in many places. Often a third shift is added to an elementary school.

Companies receive tax breaks if they sponsor an adult education program for their employees. The employer provides a classroom and pays a teacher. INEA supplies the books and the training for the teacher. In 1996-97, 696,000 adults studied in the primaria and 162,000 received a completion certificate. More than 680,000 attended the secundaria, and more than 204,000 received a certificate of completion.[22] Besides helping people within Mexico, INEA also provides textbooks for use in the United States. Chapter Six discusses these projects.

There also is a program for the military. Every 18-year-old is required to do military service on Saturdays for one year. Those who are illiterate or have not completed primary or secondary school are required to study during this period. Usually soldiers who have completed the secundaria teach the uneducated. In 1997, the year the program was started, 535 soldiers learned to read and write, 4,810 received the primaria certificate, and 13,617 received the secundaria certificate. In 1998, 36,000 soldiers tutored 79,609 recruits to receive their basic education. By the end of

1998, the military was operating programs at 144 military bases and at 994 schools.[23]

The military program typically consists of 24 units, or modules, in language, math, and science. Recruits are placed in groups of 15, with one teacher and two helpers. They follow the following schedule for 44 Saturday sessions during the year.[24]

8:00-8:20	Flag raising
8:20-9:10	Basic education (*alfabetización, primaria, or secundaria*)
9:10-9:20	Recess
9:20-10:10	Basic education
10:10-10:20	Recess
10:20-10:50	Basic education
10:50-11:50	Life skills (being 18, interpersonal relationships, AIDS, sexuality, pregnancy, family, violence, addiction, human rights, the community)
11:50-12:00	Recess
12:00-12:50	Military education (Military service, social labor, the Mexican military, patriotic symbols, public security)
12:50-1:00	Recess
1:00-1:30	Military drills
1:30-2:00	Physical education

The current model of adult education is being revised. The new version of the model will focus on making materials more relevant, improving the quality of teaching, and achieving equality in education. Education officials hope to make the program more relevant by diversifying the teaching modules and strategies for teaching, depending on the group being taught. There will be specific teaching modules for people who live in rural areas and cities and for men and women. Appropriate modules for the targeted group will be used. Better materials, better training for instructors, and more efficient bureaucracy will improve the quality of adult education. Equality in education refers to offering services to people who have historically been disenfranchised. The focus will be on women, indigenous people, and farm workers who have little or no education.

The 1998 proposal divides instruction into three segments: initial, primaria, and secundaria. Each segment is divided into language and communication, mathematics, and science. Each segment includes units that will match the interests of specific groups.

The whole system will involve 24 modules. After the basic literacy level, there is a test; and those who pass will receive a certificate. There will be an exam after each of the modules for the primaria and the secundaria. In the *alfabetización* module, the *palabra gendora* method will be used to teach reading and writing.

Adult education in Mexico has been an important theme since the time of the revolution. The expectations have increased over the years, and the current goal is to provide everyone with six years of primary schooling and three years of secondary school. Literacy campaigns were the main methods used in the past; today there is an institutionalized program run by INEA. In 1970, 91% of the population had not completed the nine years of primary and secondary school. Today that number stands at 58.6%, and major efforts are under way to reduce this number even more.

In the cities, the education system has made tremendous improvements in keeping students in school and in providing quality education for the children. The challenges of the countryside are a very different matter. There are poverty, language difficulties, and a culture of illiteracy. Officials have tried various experiments to improve the education level of the rural groups. Now that free trade agreements have increased demands for a literate population, the Mexican education authorities have been forced to step up their efforts to increase the adult literacy rate.

Notes

1. Frederico Rosas Barrera, "Vista Familiar," *Educación 2001* (January 1996): 52.

2. Paul de la Garza, "Teachers Strike Spotlights Mexico's Education Failures," *Chicago Tribune*, 22 May 1997, p. 8.

3. Secretaría de Educación Pública, *Informe de Labores 1997-98* (Mexico, 1998), p. 34.

4. Ibid., p. 35.

5. Ibid., p. 37.

6. Ibid., p. 36.

7. Etty Haydee Estevez, "La Lucha Contra el Rezago," *Educación 2001* (January 1996): 5.

8. "Education Secretary: Only One Percent of Indigenous Children Study at Universities," *The News*, Mexico City, 27 October 2001. http://www.thenewsmexico.com/noticia.asp?id=11515

9. Nicolas Cheetham, *Mexico: A Short History* (New York: Thomas Y. Crowell, 1971), p. 277.

10. Allan Riding, *Distant Neighbors* (New York: Random House, 1984), p. 288.

11. T.A. Merrill and R. Miró, *Mexico: A Country Study* (Washington: U.S. Government Printing Office, 1997), p. 97.

12. Federico Rosas Barerra, "Mexico Indigena: Un Perfil Estadístico," *Educación 2001* (December 1995): 34.

13. "Educación Indigena," *Educación 2001* (December 1995): 11.

14. Interview with Susani Justo, DGEI, in Mexico City, February 1998.

15. *Plan y Programa de Educación y Capacitación de la Mujer Indigena* (Mexico: Dirección General de Educación Indigena, 1988). Interview with Prof. Alberto Hernandez, Director of the DGEI, 21 February 1989.

16. Interview with Linguista Jose Carmen Díaz Miguel, DGEI, 15 October 1998.

17. Vincent Padgett, *The Mexican Political System* (Atlanta: Houghton-Mifflin, 1976), p. 286.

18. Mary Joan Leonard, "Anti-Illiteracy Campaign in Mexico, 1944-46," master's thesis, University of California at Berkeley, 1958, p. 61.

19. Instituto Nacional para la Educación de los Adultos, *Aprendiendo Juntos* (Mexico City: Secretariía de Educación Pública, n.d.).

20. *Informe 1987-88*, p. 145.

21. Mary Beth Sheridan, "New Welfare Initiative Up Against Price Controls," *Los Angeles Times*, Reprinted in *The News*, Mexico City, 18 January 1999.

22. *Informe 1997-98*, p. 111.
23. Rosas Barrera, op. cit., p. 35.
24. *Marco Operativo del Programa* (Mexico: Instituto Nacional para la Educación de los Adultos, 1977).

CHAPTER FOUR

SPECIAL EDUCATION

In February 1998, while I was conducting a school visit and interviewing the director, she took me to a classroom on the second floor of the school, where I met the Unidad de Servicios de Apoyo a la Educación Regular (USAER) team. Five people were meeting in the room. One was a psychologist, the second was a social worker, the third was a special education teacher, the fourth was a speech therapist, and the last one was a specialist in pedagogy. As we talked, I learned of their frustrations. Along with learning problems, they have to help the students come to terms with parental abuse, neglect, and sometimes with sexual abuse. All of these issues have a direct bearing on the teaching of literacy in the primarias. USAER is the latest attempt to deal with special education problems at the school level.

Special Education, 1867-1977

The first special education schools appeared in Mexico during the presidency of Benito Juárez. The national school for the deaf was funded in 1867, and in 1870 funds were provided for a national school for the blind. In 1914 a school in León, Guanajuato, was started for the mentally retarded. There were experiments at National Autonomous University of Mexico (UNAM) from 1919-1927 concerning techniques to educate the mentally retarded. These resulted in a model school for special education in Mexico City in 1929, and in 1932 the Departamento de Psicopedagogia e Higine Escolar became part of the SEP. By 1937, the Ley Organica de Educación (education law) contained sections to protect the mentally retarded.

To have one central place to deal with special education problems, the Clinica de Conducta in Mexico City was funded in

1937. Medical, psychological, and pedagogical resources came together to help the mentally deficient. In 1943 a school was created to train special education teachers, and by 1944 there were 10 special education schools in Mexico City. In 1966, along with the 10 special education schools in Mexico City, there were 12 special education schools in the rest of the country.

In 1970 the Dirección General de Educación Especial was created as a department of the SEP. The emphasis from 1970-1994 was on parallel programs to help those in need of special education. These programs included clinicas de conducta, special schools for each type of problem.

Special Education, 1978-1994

Special education is a program for anyone who has a physical, psychological, or social problem. Adults in prison are included in this definition. There are seven areas of special education:

1. mental deficiency
2. gifted
3. deaf
4. blind
5. learning disability
6. physically handicapped
7. behavior problems.

When this study started in 1978, the model was for a parallel program. The information that follows centers on visits to special education facilities and interviews during the 1978-1989 period.

In 1978 I visited the oldest clinica de conducta in Mexico City. The director was a doctor, and we discussed the procedure for admitting students.

If a student is not learning in the regular school, the following procedure takes place. The teacher refers the student to the director of the school who, with the zone inspector, decides if the student needs to be referred to a special clinic. Admission to the school can be denied if the parent refuses to take the student to the clinic. When parent and student arrive at the clinic, they are interviewed by a social worker. A family history is completed. The student is then given a medical examination and, if needed, an EEG. Next the student is tested by a psychologist for intelligence, perception, and emotion. A combination of tests, such as the WISC, the Bender, the Frostig, and the Draw-a-Man, are used.

The student then goes to a specialist teacher for a battery of learning tests. The *Prueba VISAM* is a test that measures verbal skills, intellectual ability, social maturity, emotional level, and motor control. The *Prueba Psicipedagogica de Detección de Problemas Aprendizaje* (Psychological Test to Detect Learning Problems) measures visual perception, motor skills, letter discrimination, spatial orientation, phonics, comprehension, conceptualization, and sequence. The ABC test by Lorenzo Fihlo measures reading skills. Teachers do not use all of the tests with each student.

After the testing is completed, there is a staff conference to discuss the course of action. Then the parents are notified, and the psychologist explains the results. Possibilities for treatment include a special class within the local school, a special program at the clinic, or referral to a special school.[1]

After I left the clinica de conducta, I visited a school for children with mongolism. In one school in Mexico City, the day consists of four and a half hours of activities. The day begins with discipline activities. It is common for students to line up and then march to the classroom. Next, the students are inspected for hygiene. This is followed by psychomotor activities. Training in writing and language skills is done with Frostig materials. Social habits are the next order of business, with time being spent on toilet training, eating habits, and other survival skills. Perceptual and motor skills are taught last.

My next stop was the Instituto Medico Pedagógico, the oldest school for the educationally handicapped in Mexico City. Students with IQs from 70 to 105 are admitted to this school. Along with the regular teaching staff, the school has a doctor, a dentist, a social worker, a speech therapist, a psychologist, and a music teacher. The main duties of the doctor are to check for physical problems and to evaluate students who arrive with their parents. These are students who have not been referred from a clinic. In 1978, 30% to 40% of the students at the school had emotional problems, 15% to 20% were hyperactive, and the rest had physical problems, such as epilepsy.

The psychologist and the speech therapist work with students in the school. In addition to working with individual students, the psychologist is in charge of the testing program. The speech therapist spends 30 minutes per week with the students who have problems. Most of the therapy concerns articulation and stuttering.

In the classroom, students are divided into three primary school grades — first, second, and third — with each grade lasting two years. The emphasis of the school is on discipline, perceptual activities, oral fluency, and reading using a phonetic approach. Frostig materials are used in the lower grades. Government textbooks are used with the older students.

In 1980 the emphasis shifted to special education classes based in the primarias. Programs were also provided to try to increase the retention rate.[2] This meant that a significant portion of available resources were (and still are) used to help "normal" students learn. When I visited in 1989, 60 researchers were examining how children learn. Two experimental programs that showed promise were being used in selected schools.

The first program, based on the work of American researcher Joseph Renzulli, was for gifted students. The experiment was designed to last for two academic school years, with a total of 42 schools used in the study. It has been so successful that the timeframe has been extended, and many states are contemplating using this program. In this program the teachers, the principal, and the students pick gifted students in either grades three and four or grades five and six. The students are pulled out of class two times per week to work with the school psychologist. When the students are in the program, they determine their interests, visit places, and see movies. Students are grouped by interests; and in the second stage of the program, the students develop a community project. They investigate the problem and then develop a plan of action. In stage three, the students carry out the plan.

The curriculum is geared to the average student, and this is an attempt to challenge the brighter students. One researcher from the department of special education supervises every four psychologists assigned to the schools in the program.

The second experimental program is designed to increase learning through the use of color-coded activity cards. White cards are for general readiness skills. The pink cards contain group activities. Blue cards contain prereading activities. Yellow cards contain beginning reading activities, and the green cards are designed to help students work with the written language. Before teachers are given the cards, there is a training program; and a staff member at each school has been assigned to help the teachers use the cards. During my visits to the various schools, I asked the teachers about the cards. Everyone had their cards, but few used them.

During my 1989 visits I met a special education teacher assigned to the schools. She worked on reading and writing with three groups in three different schools. The materials she used were from Frostig, and the model of learning was based on Swiss child psychologist Jean Piaget's studies. The teacher visited each school two days per week, and the students were pulled out of class to work with her. In terms of training, she went to the normal superior and majored in pedagogy. When I met her, she had been working in this aspect of the program for three years, and the project was four years old.

Two other programs designed to reduce the failure rate need to be mentioned. The *grupos integrados* program began in the special education department in 1970-71. In this program, students who fail the first grade go to a special class to repeat the grade. Students from several schools attend the class. The special class receives help from a psychologist, a language teacher, and a social worker, as well as the regular teacher. Although the students repeat the materials, this extra help has reduced the failure rate. Statistics from 1976-81 show that the passing rate of students in this program is about 70%.[3]

The last program to reduce the failure rate is a combined fifth- and sixth-grade class. Students who are between 12 to 15 years old can enter this class. The important lessons from the fifth grade are taught during the first semester of the sixth-grade year. During the second semester, the important lessons of the sixth grade are taught. This allows the students to catch up and graduate with their respective classes.

Special Education, 1995-2000

The 1995-2000 plan calls for an integrated program in which the students are helped in their regular classes.[4] Mexican educators want to integrate special education services into the regular school program, but they also recognize the need to treat more than one problem. For example, the student with a hearing problem might also have behavior problems.

The number of individuals with special education problems increased in all categories since 1993. Autism was added to the list in 1997.

During this period, more than 316,000 students with special education problems have been helped. Most special education services are at the state level. In 1993 there were 741 special education schools, as contrasted with only 100 schools by 2000. In 1993 there were 585 centers for psychological problems. This number in 2000 was reduced to 35 centers. In place of the schools and programs are centers that focus on multiple problems. In 2000 there were 1,200 such centers.

The new emphasis is reflected in the USAER program. As of 2000, there were 2,105 functioning USAER units in the schools. From my experience, the quality of the program varies from school to school.

A USAER team consists of a psychologist, a language teacher, and a social worker. Specialists are brought into the group depending on the needs of the schools. Each USAER group serves five schools and is responsible for working with students, their parents, and the teachers in the school. Within each school are

74

one or more special education teachers that deal with interventions when the team is not present.

When the teacher, the director of the school, or the parents feel that USAER can help a student, an initial evaluation is conducted. Depending on the type of problem, various evaluation instruments are used. There are questionnaires for the parents and the teacher, as well as tests and observations of the student. The USAER team then decides on a plan of action. Usually this involves tasks that the parents must do at home. As part of the plan, members of the USAER team will see the student either once or twice per week.

As I previously stated, the centers for special education have a new purpose in the 1995-2000 plan. On 28 September 1998 I visited the clinica de conducta described in the first section of this chapter. This is the only clinica de conducta in Mexico that specializes in dyslexia, bed-wetting, physical abuse, sexual abuse, and ADHD. There are two shifts with 13 psychologists and psychiatrists and nine specialists in pedagogy. They see 300 students per shift per month.

When a student is referred from the school, they take the WISC-C and the Bender tests. If there is a neurological problem, the student is referred to a hospital. Also, the staff administers teacher-made tests and develops a program. Group therapy, individual therapy, and family therapy are available. Usually the therapy is for one hour per week. The staff of the clinic maintains contact with the school. Formerly, medical personnel were part of the clinic. However, they were removed from the clinic because of budget restrictions. People bring their children from throughout Mexico City to attend the clinic.[5]

The commitment to help students with special needs has existed since the mid-1800s. Special education in Mexico has developed from a few specialized schools to a program designed to maximize the learning potential of each student in the regular school environment.

Notes

1. Interview with Profesora Guadalupe Gracida, the director of special education, Lic.; Elke Lort, head of psychological services; and Dr. Jaime Rodriquez Hernández, the director of the Clinica de Conducta, 4-5 September 1978.
2. *La Educación Especial en México* (Mexico: Dirección General de Educación Especial, 1981), Chapter 1.
3. "Estadisticas — Educación Especial." http://www.sep.gob.mx
4. The new plan is presented in six very small volumes. *Proyecto General para la Educación Especial en México, Cuadernos de Integración Educativa No.1; Articulo 41 Comentado de la Ley General de Educación, Cuandernos de Integración Educativa No. 2; Declaración de Salamanca de Principios, Politica y Practica para las Necesidades Educativas Especiales, Cuadernos de Integración Educative No. 3; Unidad de Servicios de Apoyo a la Educación Regular (USAER), Cuadernos de Integración Educativa No. 4; La Integración Educativa como Fundamento de la Calidad del Sistema de Educación Basica para Todos, Cuadernos de Integración Educativa No. 5; Proyecto General para la Educación Especial Pautas de Organización, Cuadernos de Integración, Cuadernos de Integración Educativa No. 6.*
5. Interview with Proffessor Alberto Laguna Valencia, Clinica de Conducta, Mexico City, 28 September 1998.

CHAPTER FIVE

TEACHER TRAINING

The 970 students at Maestra Queta's school were excited about being able to go home early because of the first faculty meeting of the year. After the students left, the school's 14 male and eight female teachers came into the meeting room. There was a 10-minute delay until the meeting was called to order and the director read the charge for the group, then the faculty elected a secretary and selected a representative from each grade to serve on an advisory committee. These teachers were expected to report information to the other teachers in their respective grades.

There were several committees in this school, and each teacher was appointed to a committee. After the director read the committee assignments, there was a discussion because the teacher in charge of ceremonies wanted to be on the cleanliness committee, and the teacher on the first aid committee wanted to do something else. Finally, after 10 minutes, the problem was resolved.

Campus cleanliness was the next major issue. The principal was concerned because the campus was littered with papers after the break. He announced that a slogan and poster campaign would begin immediately so that the condition of the campus would improve. All teachers were expected to play a role in the campaign — this was an extra duty, along with the committee assignments. After another long discussion, it was decided that each teacher also would have the additional duty of selling food at break for three weeks during the year.

The last item on the agenda was a directive from the dirección on grading procedures. It was decided by the dirección that the teachers should send home a monthly progress report on each student. (All schools in Mexico City eventually adopted this plan.) This created a stir, and everyone started to talk at once. The discussion then led to the problems that teachers have with students. One teacher blamed the whole situation on television. Another blamed the situation on parental pressure — parents demanding that students pass to the next grade though the requirements have not been met. A group of teachers felt that the system is responsible for the inability of all the students to achieve at maximum levels. It was 12:30 p.m., and many teachers started to leave.

This faculty meeting took place in September 1978, but the issues and the discussions are still the same in Mexico. Most of these issues also are reflected in faculty meetings in schools across the United States.

The treatment and training of the classroom teacher is central to the education system and to the teaching of literacy. Well-trained teachers can motivate, teach, and handle the education needs of the students, as well as perform the nonteaching tasks required by the bureaucracy. The Mexican system has an orderly, well-developed plan for teacher training. Because literacy is the responsibility of the primary school, I will discuss teacher training programs only for this level.

Teacher training includes several parts. The first of these parts is the program to train and prepare new teachers for the primary school. Since 1984, a plan has been in place to train experienced teachers who have only nine years of basic education and four years in the normal school. This plan consists of training at UPN (Universidad Pedegogica Nacional), at teacher centers, and in a bold program called the Carrerra Magisterial.

Financial incentives, union rules, and the tension between labor and management all affect the performance of teachers and administrators. I will take up these parts of the teacher training picture later in this chapter.

The Normal School

Mexican educators have long held the opinion that the professional status of educators should be raised.[1] While teacher education in most industrialized countries is part of higher education or university studies, in Mexico it occurs at a level equivalent to an intermediate or senior high school. Teacher training for primary school teachers is done in normal schools. Secondary teachers attend the normal superior.

Before 1984 a prospective primary school teacher had to attend six years in the primary school, three years in the secondary school, and then four years in the normal school. In September 1984 the requirements were changed, and an additional three years of preparatory school were required before the candidate could enter the normal school. The first class graduated in June 1988 with the *licenciatura*, the equivalent of a B.A. degree.

This change caused a radical restructuring of the curriculum. The old curriculum was designed for students who were 15 years old when they began their teacher-training program. This curriculum emphasized basic skills, such as three years of math, Spanish, natural science, social science, and physical education. In the fourth year, they analyzed the official program and the books used in the schools. They also took courses in administration, legislation, and social and economic problems of Mexico. In addition, they did observations and practice teaching in the schools during each year of the program.

The new curriculum for the Benemerita Escuela Nacional de Maestros in Mexico City became the curriculum for normal schools throughout the country. Under this curriculum, entering students must complete 12 years of schooling and then take an exam to enter the normal school. The normal school students are placed into groups, and the teachers rotate. Students spend approximately 32 hours per week in the normal school. During the first year, they take courses in the philosophical and legal bases of the school system, the history of education, problems and politics, teaching mathematics, content of the curriculum, teaching Spanish, development of the child, and strategies for studying and communication. They also take a course in the social context of schools and spend time observing in a classroom.

The second year focuses on the economic development of Mexico, teaching mathematics, teaching Spanish, education specialties, pedagogy, regional issues, and teaching natural science, geography, history, physical education, and art. Students observe classes and practice teaching in a school.

The third year involves courses in pedagogy, the formation of etiquette and civic duty, and teaching natural science, geography, history, physical education, and art. Students also study planning and evaluation of teaching, and they observe and practice teaching in a school. The fourth year includes working in a school for 28 hours per week and a four-hour seminar to discuss the teaching experience. This is done in both semesters.[2]

Preparing prospective teachers in Mexico is very different from the sort of preparation teachers receive in the United States. For one thing, there is a national curriculum, and every primary school student in the country uses the same textbooks. Thus the teachers are learning how to use the actual materials that they will have in the classroom. The emphasis in Mexican teacher training is on the physical, cognitive, and emotional development of the students. Prospective teachers examine the various methods of teaching literacy with an emphasis on oral expression.

Another major objective is to help the future teacher to be creative and not to rely on repetitive activities and memorization. Teacher training is intended to create teachers who: 1) have intellectual curiosity and can express themselves both orally and in writing, 2) know the contents of the program of study, 3) know how to involve students with various learning strategies, 4) are professional and ethical, and 5) understand and respond to the social conditions of the students in the school.

There is a school on the campus of the Escuela Nacional where students preparing to become teachers have the opportunity to practice their skills. They also can do this in schools in the community. It is interesting that the main function of the Escuela Nacional is to train teachers and not to weed out candidates, as is common in the United States. For example, when students are found to have drug or alcohol problems, they are given therapy.

Instructors at the normal school do not need prior teaching experience in the primary school. The only requirement is that they have a college degree in a specific area. Many have graduate degrees in education.[3]

In 1978 the *Escuela Nacional* had an enrollment of 5,920 students, divided into 82 groups in the morning and 66 in the afternoon. Since the stricter requirements went into effect, there has been a drastic decrease in enrollment. The class of 1987, who still were under the old system, had an enrollment of 1,005 students, who were divided into 33 groups. The class of 1988 had only 151 students in five groups; the class of 1990 had 181 students divided into 10 groups.[4] In September 1999 there were 1,500 students.

An article in *Educación 2001* (September 1995) profiled the normal school students for the 1994-95 school year. From 83% to 85% attended public schools (primarias, secundarias, and the media superior school); and 13.8% received a general preparation diploma, 66.9% received a diploma in pedagogy, and the rest received their diplomas in social sciences, humanities, technology, or agriculture. Almost 60% lived with their parents, and only 4.2% of their fathers and 1.9% of their mothers had attended the university. About 25% of the parents did not complete primary school.[5]

When I began my research, the teachers complained that the normal school students were immature (they entered the normal school at age 15). Now, a prospective teacher must complete the same number of years in a media superior school as a student who prepares for a career in law or medicine. However, the normal school instructors have stated privately that the current group of teachers is deficient in their academic skills.

I spent substantial amounts of time in classrooms in 1978-79, 1988-89, and 1998-99. In 1978 all of the teachers I observed had only 13 years of schooling, compared to 1998-99, when the majority had 16 years. Does more formal education create better teachers? This is a very difficult question to answer. In 1978 I watched some excellent teaching. Many teachers were project-oriented, and the classrooms buzzed with activity. Discipline was excellent. In 1998-99 I saw the same types of things. The teachers were connected to the students. I have a vivid image of one teacher squatting on the floor with the students and playing a game.

Mexican society has changed in the last 20 years. Now, there are more family problems, such as divorce and drugs. Thus the teacher's job is more difficult. I strongly believe that good teaching is the interaction between love of the profession, education attainment, and experience. In my opinion, more formal education is not the main factor in creating better teachers.

Universidad Pedagógica Nacional

Organized in 1978, the Universidad Pedagógica Nacional (UPN) is an attempt to improve teachers' skills. There is at least one branch of the university in each state, and curriculum and policies are controlled from the main university campus located in Mexico City.

UPN offers six degrees that are the equivalent of a bachelor of arts degree. The first degree is in basic education. Only teachers working in preschools or primary schools can apply. The second degree is in adult education and is open to graduates of normal schools and to people who are working in adult education. The third degree is in education administration. Next is a degree that trains specialists in pedagogy to design, implement, and evaluate education programs. The last two programs are for school psychologists and school sociologists. Along with these programs, teachers can take courses to become specialists in math and language.

All students in the six programs take basic education courses that include methods of research, Mexican society, history of ideas, and mathematics. Social functions of education, statistics, political education, problems of education, and education in the society form the next strand. After completing these courses, the students take courses in their area of specialization.

On 3 October 1988, UPN introduced specialization courses that take three semesters to complete. To enroll in these programs, the individual must have the equivalent of a B.A. degree. The specializations are in planning, developing, and evaluating curriculum; mathematics; language; and theory and models of teaching.

The requirements that new teachers must have a B.A. degree forced a change in the focus of the university. Currently there are 76 branches with approximately 20,000 students, of whom 4,000 are on the main campus in Mexico City. These institutions train students to be administrators or to do work outside the classroom. UPN has a research section that offers a master's degree in Spanish, math, history, science, or multicultural education. When I interviewed university officials in fall 1998, UPN representatives stated that there would be a Ph.D. program in conjunction with Simon Fraser University in Canada. Also, they have a bilingual certification program with California State University at San Diego. At the time of the interview, there were 10 students in the program, and they studied for one year in California and one year in Mexico.[6]

At the main campus in Mexico City in 1998, 558 students were working to obtain the *licenciatura* in education administration, 1,569 were working for a degree in educational pedagogy, 1,454 were studying psychology, 229 were studying sociology, and 122 were studying for a degree in indigenous education. There were 248 students working for master's degrees, and 233 were receiving training in various specializations.[7]

Currently, there is a debate about the purpose of the UPN. Many people feel that its responsibilities can be handled by other parts of the SEP. By looking at the history of the Universidad Pedagógica Nacional, we can begin to understand the forces that shape Mexican education. The SEP wanted a small university based in Mexico City that was independent of the union, had a small administrative staff, and offered courses for students from the normal and media superior levels. It would offer specializations, master's degrees, doctorates, and teaching-at-a-distance programs. There would be a maximum of 30,000 students. The teacher's union wanted a big university, with a rector under the union and many divisions. Graduates of the normal school would attend, and the school would offer traditional degrees with a traditional organization found in every state. The result was constant disagreement about the mission of the UPN; and in the last 17 years, there have been 11 directors.[8]

The Mexico City campus reflects the union's view of the university. It is located in the southern part of Mexico City and contains lots of stone buildings on a hillside. When entering the campus, the students walk up a large number of stone steps to reach the classrooms. The administrative offices and the library are at the bottom of the hill. It is impressive.

Requiring new teachers to have more education than those already teaching may cause dissent. In the target schools used in this study, few teachers have chosen to go to the UPN. Instead, many have gone to the normal superior (the training school for secondary teachers) in the morning and are working the second shift in a secondary school. There would be less than 1,000 pesos (less than one percent of a teacher's salary) difference between a new teacher with a degree working two shifts in the primary school and a 15-year veteran working one turn in the primary school and one turn in the secondary school.

There also is a movement to build secondary schools. In 1978-79, there were only 7,857 secondary schools in the country. During the 1986-87 school year, there were 16,513 secondary schools; and 26,710 were functioning during the 1998-99 school year.[9] This situation has created more employment for primary school teachers who have completed specialized courses at the normal superior.

Teacher Centers

ProNAP (the national program to help teachers working in basic education) is the agency responsible for providing workshops, courses, books for teachers, and teacher centers. The goal is to improve the quality of currently employed teachers. As of August 2000, 505 teacher centers were in operation throughout Mexico. To become a director of a teacher center, the person must present a project to the department of the SEP responsible for the center.

I visited the teacher center at the Escuela Normal on 16 October 1998. The center consists of a library (books, videos, audiotapes, CDs) with television monitors and computers. Teachers can check materials out or use them in the center. However, the budget is small, and so most centers do not have much material. Lessons can be developed on the computer.

When several teachers express a need, the director of the center can offer a course on a subject of interest. During the months of November and December 1998, the center at the Escuela Normal sponsored many activities. There were a movie program — a video every week that lasted for two hours — and a three-session workshop on making things for the classroom. There were an exhibition of paintings and a concert. To meet requirements for the Carrera Magisterial, three courses were offered: prevention of addiction, sexual education, and the health of adolescents. Finally, a series of workshops was held, including: the teaching of mathematics, construction of objects to foster critical thinking, psychodrama, the relationship of music to the other arts, a tour to the Templo Mayor museum, and creating a student museum.[10] All of these activities were designed to help teachers in the classroom. The center also provided a place for teachers to meet with their friends and to be entertained. Fifty-four percent of the teachers responding to the questionnaires indicated that a teacher center was near their schools. However, only 39% used centers. The centers are only a few years old, and it may take a while to gain the interest of the teachers.

Teacher Compensation, Benefits, and the Carerra Magisterial

As part of the 1992 emergency plan for education, a program was devised to increase the skills of classroom teachers. The teachers receive pay increases as they move up the scale in the Carerra Magisterial. Moving up involves evaluation of five factors: time in service, academic grade, professional preparation, courses, and working beyond what is required in the field. Each area is assigned points. The entry level is A, and this is accomplished with nine hours of extra classes. When teachers take courses and agree to have their class evaluated, they move to level B. And the progression continues. The final level is E, and the minimum time required to reach this level is 14 years. Teachers at level A receive five times the minimum salary, level B six times, level C nine times, level D 11 times, and level E 14 times.[11] (The minimum salary is equivalent to about US$4.00 per day, and it takes about three minimum salaries to survive in Mexico City.) The beginning salary for teachers in Mexico City currently is 4.03 times the minimum salary, or US$6,676.00. Several extra incentives such as December bonuses are included in the salary total. Of the teachers answering the survey, 50% were in level A, 16% in level B, 2% in level C, and 32% did not answer the question. During my 2001 visit, several directors told me that teachers were stalled at certain levels because their students were not making the expected progress.

Teacher compensation and benefits are always important to the quality of education and the teaching workforce. Organized labor plays an important role, just as it does in the United States. Every person employed by the school system is required to join the Sindicato Nacional de Trabajadores Educativo (National Syndicate of Educational Workers, SNTE), which is the union. The Secretarío de Educación Pública appoints teachers. They have tenure from the time they are first hired and can be removed only through resignations, abandonment of employment, mental health, physical disability, or death. The union negotiates a nationwide salary schedule and adjusts this amount according to the cost of living in each area.

Until the election of Carlos Salinas in 1988, the Partido Revolucionario Institucional (PRI) controlled labor by using labor bosses, or *caciques.* These bosses guaranteed votes from the members of their labor unions in exchange for favors from the government. After he was elected, Salinas ordered the arrest of the head of the oil worker's union; and this action started the downfall of the caciques. For 25 years, Carlos Jungitud Barrios ran the teacher's union (SNTE). Opposition to his policies was suppressed and resentment grew in the country. In 1989, 300,000 teachers marched in Mexico City to topple Carlos Jungitud Barrios. The teachers demanded democracy and better salaries. By the end of that year Jungitud was replaced by Esther Gordilla.

Gordilla, appointed by Salinas, agreed to all of the changes in the modernization program. However, there were locals within the organization that disagreed with the modernization, and there were teachers who raised serious questions about the program. Section 10 of the teacher's union, which consisted of primary school teachers in Mexico City, objected to the modernization program because it created eight pay grades based on academic preparation and performance. Their concern was that people would be promoted unfairly.

During the 1992-93 school year, the union paid teachers to go to Mexico City and discuss issues concerning education. A new group came every week; and on Tuesday, 16 June 1992, I met with one of these groups. The teachers were from the states of Guanajuato, México, Nuevo León, Chiapas, Tamaulipas, Tabasco, and Michoacán. There was concern because the government would not reveal its new plan until the last two weeks in August and because of a discrepancy between the pay of teachers in state schools and in federal schools. They wondered how long it would take to equalize the pay. Some teachers felt that it would take up to five years for this pay equalization to occur. Also of concern was that some non-PRI state governors would not receive enough money to run their schools. And because the teachers had used one method of instruction for 14 years, they were concerned about the new methods. Finally, the teachers also expressed concern because the president had indicated that 3.5 times the minimum wage was equal to a professional salary. Five or six times the minimum wage would allow a person to live modestly.

Because there is more democracy in the union, there also is more freedom and thus many strikes. In May 1997, 50,000 striking teachers from throughout the country marched in Mexico City to have their wages doubled. This was at a time when the government was facing a financial crisis. Occasionally, sections of the union go on strike. There also is division within the umbrella organization, the SNTE. Many locals are run by the CNTE, and this group is more radical than the SNTE. Sometimes these strikes have to deal with political issues within the union. Also, it is not uncommon for the government to interfere with the election process within the union. For example, in July 1998 Federal District Local 9 of the SNTE held elections for its nine-member council. The national leadership tried to pack the council with five non-CNTE sympathizers, though the CNTE had controlled Local 9 since 1989. A group of CNTE members entered the Senate Chamber to discuss their grievances with a group of senators. Six weeks later, these individuals were arrested on charges of theft, rioting, and kidnapping. Thousands of teachers marched, gridlocking Mexico City. Finally the charges for kidnapping and robbery were dropped, and the teachers were free on bail of more than 160,000 pesos.[12]

Although states now have the primary responsibility for education, there are still protests at the federal level. A national salary is set by the SEP, but a discrepancy between the federal schools and state schools still exists in the poorer states. For example, in 2001 teachers in Mexico City earned $750 dollars a month and teachers in the old state schools in Chiapas earned as little as $270 dollars a month.[13]

On 15 May 2001, about 5,000 teachers started to protest for higher wages. Most of the teachers were from the poorer states of Oaxaca, Chiapas, Michoacán, and Guerrero. The strike ended on June 14, and the teachers accepted an 11% raise that had already been offered. The government of Vincente Fox did not budge from its previous offer.

Teachers must pay social security, union dues based on time worked, and maternity pay and must make payments to the Instituto de Seguridad y Servicos Sociales para los Trabajadores del Estado (ISSTE). This last provides medical services, low cost loans, and merchandise and travel discounts. Teachers receive pay throughout the summer and 20 days of pay in December. They also receive an extra 20 days of pay in January. (This number is negotiable and changes with the union contracts. In some areas it is 45 days.)

There are drawbacks to this system. In 1989 teachers in Mexico City were given the month of January off because of the high levels of smog. Also, classroom time was lost because of a union dispute. The teachers were required to teach until August 15 to make up the lost time. Typically, when a teacher is sick, if a substitute can be found, then the class continues. If not, the class is canceled and the students are sent home.

Views of the Teachers

In May 1998 an article appeared in *Educación 2001* concerning the results of surveys done in April 1997 and April 1998 that compared citizens' views regarding schools with teachers' views. Four hundred people were questioned by telephone in April of 1998. The first question asked about the quality of public education. Forty-one percent said that it was very good, 23% said average, and 33% said poor. The comparable results for April 1998 were 31%, 22%, and 40% respectively. Another question asked whether the teachers were well prepared. In 1997, 57% said they were well prepared, 16% said average, and 16% said poorly prepared. The comparable numbers for 1998 were 64%, 20%, and 13%.[14] Almost two-thirds of the people rated the education system as good or average. Approximately 85% of the respondents rated the teachers as well prepared or average.

In the study that forms the basis for this book, the teachers were asked to rate their schools and the education system as a whole. Sixty-four percent rated their schools as good or excellent, and 38% rated the system as good or excellent. The second series of questions concerned the training of teachers. About 40% of the teachers had the *licencetura* (1998-99), and about 10% were taking classes in the university. About 54% of the teachers worked near a teacher center, and 60.8% said that they did not use the teacher centers. Only 21% of the teachers indicated that they did not receive training in their schools (1998-99). During the

1988-89 school year, 64% of the teachers felt that the increased education levels for teachers would not help. During the 1998-99 school year, only three percent felt this way.

From interviews with teachers and directors, the most important changes in the past 20 years have been improvement in the quality of the textbooks and the curriculum, greater freedom allowed teachers through the use of the avance programáticos, and increased parent involvement in the schools.

Improving the quality of the teaching staff in Mexico has been a major undertaking. The government has required more education, provided training through UPN and teacher centers, and has provided financial incentives. It will take a long time for the results to be known, but indicators show a trend toward better teaching practices.

Notes

1. Isaias Alvarez Garcia, *A Search for New Alternatives in the Eduacación of Mexico's Future Primary School Teachers* (Cambridge, Mass.: Harvard University Press, 1983).
2. "Licenciatura en Educación Primaria, Mapa Curricular." This is a one-page document provided by the normal school. A copy of this document also can be found in *Educación 2001* (March 1999): 34.
3. Interview with Rodolfo Méndez Balderas, Escuela Nacional de Maestros, 16 October 1998.
4. Interview with Miguel Huerta Maldonado, Director of the Benemerita Escuela Nacional de Maestros, Mexico City, 28 February 1989.
5. Marcelino Guzmán Cota, "Perfil del Estudiante de Normal," *Educación 2001* (September 1995): 22-24.
6. Interview with Eduardo Mancera Martinez and Margarita Ruiz de Velasco Padierna, UPN, October 1998.
7. "Entrevista con Jesús Liceaga," *Educación 2001* (March 1999): 12.
8. "Pasado, Presente y Futuro de la UPN," *Educación 2001* (September 1997): 28.
9. *Estadísticas de Educación, Cuaderno Numero 6* (Mexico: Instituto Nacional de Estadística Geograpfía e Informática, 2000), pp. 16-18.

10. Published schedule for November and December 1998 plan at the teacher's center in the Escuela Normal.

11. "Programa Nacional de Carrera Magisterial," Secretaría de Educación Pública. http://www.sep.gob.mx

12. "Hunger Strikers Gives Teacher's Side of Story," *The News*, 31 January 1999. http://thenewsmexico.com

13. "Teacher's Union Accepts Pay Raise," *The News*, 16 May 2001, p. 2.

14. Roy Campos Esquerra, "La Sociedad Juzga a los Maestros," *Educación 2001* (May 1998): 27-33.

CHAPTER SIX

SPANISH LITERACY FOR MEXICANS IN THE UNITED STATES

Before NAFTA, Mexico was very reluctant to share its education system with the world. My experience with various Mexican officials confirms this attitude. In 1978 I wrote several letters to the SEP for permission to conduct a study on the teaching of reading and writing in the Mexican public schools. The SEP failed to respond. In June 1978 I went in person to the SEP and received assurances that the staff would help me with the study, which would begin at the start of the new school year in September. I also toured the Textbook Commission facility. When I returned in September, officials from the Consejo Técnico de la Educación interrogated me about the purpose of my study. For three days, I answered questions. At the end of October, after waiting for almost a month, I finally received permission to do the study. Official orders came, and I presented information about my study at each school. There was a reluctance to share "official" information.

Two years later came another example of this reluctance. In 1980 the Association of Mexican-American Educators held a conference in Mexico City. Mexican teachers were supposed to share their experiences with teachers from the United States. However, officials from the SEP outnumbered the few Mexican teachers who attended the conference, and many people felt that it was basically a U.S. conference held in Mexico.

The relationship between Mexico and the United States is changing. Since 1978 and the passage of NAFTA, the Mexican-U.S. relationship has changed tremendously. Mexican educators regularly work in classrooms in the United States, Mexican researchers make presentations at conferences, there are associations with U.S. universities, and there are state and national agreements. There are conferences featuring individuals from these countries. On the political level, people of Latin American descent hold more than 5,000 political seats in the United States.[1] The first official trip of a newly elected President George W. Bush was to Mexico to visit President Vincente Fox. Mexico and the United States have reached several agreements concerning education. These agreements focus on improving literacy and the schooling of Mexican immigrants in the United States and involve national, state, and local governments and even private agencies.

On the U.S. side of the border, the agreements have been made with individual school districts, Mexican-American organizations, programs for migrant education, state departments of education, universities, and to a limited extent the U.S. Department of Education. The agreements usually involve relatively small numbers of individuals, and so they do not receive widespread media attention, even in national publications dedicated to education. However, when we examine these programs together, we see that the Mexican government has a substantial presence in education programs in many parts of the United States.

Mexico recognizes its duty to protect its citizens living in another country, including the rights of Mexican immigrants in the United States. Mexico has 40 consulates in the United States, and such Mexican organizations as the social security administration and the adult education program work to help Mexican nationals in the United States. Also, there is the growing influence of nongovernmental forces, including those associated with bilingual trade and with pressure groups, which can force the U.S. Congress and state legislative bodies to pass laws favorable to Mexico. NAFTA was one example.

One advantage of helping immigrants in the United States is that these immigrants send money to improve villages and rural areas in Mexico. Also, by encouraging close ties with Mexican nationals, Mexico ensures that their U.S.-born children will maintain a bond with Mexico.[2]

Following are some of the education agreements and programs between Mexico and the United States, including those at the national, state, and local levels. I also discuss some of the agreements between Mexico and private agencies.

National Projects

The education agreements between Mexico and the United States are the results of a long and complicated process. The Echeverría administration (1970-76) made attempts to meet with Mexican-American leaders to strengthen ties with Mexico, but differences among the organizations in the United States prevented any institutional relationship from developing. President López Portillo (1976-82) did meet with Mexican-American organizations, and this started the work in the United States.[3]

Under the leadership of Graciela Orozco and, later, Roberto López, both of whom worked for the Ministry of Education, the number of programs with the United States increased. Mexican teachers went to Los Angeles and Louisiana. Training programs were held for bilingual teachers from the Los Angeles area. Bilingual programs in San Jose, California, used Mexican textbooks; and Mexican officials became visiting scholars in the United States. The Office of International Relations in the SEP was in charge of these programs.[4]

In February 1990 President Carlos Salinas created the Program for Mexican Communities Abroad to link Mexican communities in the United States to Mexico. Mexican consulates throughout the United States administer the program and have established nonprofit Mexican cultural institutes. These institutes exist in 23 U.S. cities, and their objectives are to promote business, tourism, culture, exhibits, artistic events, academic exchanges, scholarships, training for bilingual teachers, adult education programs, migrant education, medical insurance for U.S.-based Mexican workers, sports, and housing.[5]

Each month the list of projects related to education grows. The program was supplying Mexican textbooks for use in elementary and preschools in 1992. In addition, literacy and adult education materials were sent to U.S. cities and states, including Dallas and Brownsville, Texas; Chicago; Philadelphia; Fresno, San Francisco, Sacramento, and Los Angeles in California; and the state of Michigan. In Madera County, California, textbooks in the indigenous language Mixtec are helping Mixtec farmworkers to become literate.[6] In 1990 the SEP sent 26 Mexican teachers to work for two years in bilingual programs in Chicago. As of September 1993, 21 teachers remained; and there were plans to increase this number.[7]

In a July 1997 interview with Sofia Orozco (subdirector of the program for Mexican communities abroad), she stated that the bilingual exchange program began in 1995. In the first year, 70 teachers were sent to 14 cities. Each Mexican state was assigned a quota, and then committees were formed to pick the teachers. The teachers stayed in the United States from four to six weeks and served as teacher aides in summer-school classes. The receiving U.S. district paid the airfare and housing costs. The district also provided a stipend of $100 to $200 per week for each teacher. Afterward, U.S. teachers visited Mexico for one or two weeks. They went to schools, observed, and sometimes worked in Mexican classrooms. The visits could occur at any time during the year.

In 1997 Mexican teachers were in several cities: Detroit (16 teachers), Atlanta (17), Los Angeles (two), Portland (11), Denver (12), Sacramento (four), Philadelphia (one), Washington (one), El Paso (three), Orlando (seven), San Jose (eight), Chicago (50), St. Louis (six), Seattle (six), San Antonio (eight), San Francisco (10), and Austin (two).[8]

Mexican educators also attended the annual conferences of the National Association for Bilingual Education. At the conference in 1991, Mexican educators spoke on theories of bilingual education; and at the 1992 conference they spoke on the new program of modernization and aspects of teaching the Spanish language.[9] The same themes were repeated at the conferences of the California Association for Bilingual Education. During the 1993

California conference, 40 specialists from 25 Mexican education institutions organized displays and presented workshops on education in Mexico. Mexican educators also participated in the 1992 and 1993 conferences held by the Texas Association for Bilingual Education. Currently, it is routine to have speakers from Mexico at these conferences.

The Program for Mexican Communities Abroad developed courses for bilingual teachers in the United States. Courses are offered to districts through Mexican Cultural Centers. Each course is five sessions of six hours each for a total of 30 hours. The courses include basic and intermediate Spanish, Mexican culture and civilization, and bicultural classroom interaction.[10]

The Mexican Foreign Service is the umbrella organization that coordinates the services of the various Mexican programs in the United States. However, the programs have no central organization in the United States, and the lack of such organization leads to some duplication of effort. Indeed, most people are unaware of the many activities in which the Mexican education establishment is involved in the United States.

On 17 August 1990, U.S. Education Secretary Lauro Cavazos and Mexican Secretary of Public Education Manuel Bartlett Díaz signed a memorandum of understanding, establishing closer ties on education issues and programs. The agreement remained in effect until 31 December 1991, with provision for successive two-year extensions.

The original agreement included a stipulation for holding a border conference in October 1991 to discuss the teaching of English in Mexico and of Spanish in the United States, as well as teacher exchanges, migrant education, education administration, education research, innovation, and improvement of intercultural understanding. The conference focused on technological education, teacher education, and professional development. More than 500 people attended, with each of the border states sending a delegation.[11]

The activities for 1992-93 included exchanges of professors and researchers, an examination of ways to decrease dropout rates, open education programs for Mexicans living in the United

States, summer courses in Mexico, help for migrant students, joint efforts in environmental education, linking U.S. and Mexican universities, improving technical education in both countries, and sending Mexican teachers to study in U.S. education institutions.

On 21 June 1993 the Mexican and U.S. Secretaries of Education met and signed an annex to the agreement. In October 1993 they met again in Ciudad Juárez, and the conference focused on the professional development of teachers. Another meeting was held in November 1996. In 1998, the activities planned for 1998-2000 focused on the areas of sharing information, special education, school-to-work programs, adult education, literacy, and cooperation in higher education. Table 5 summarizes the national and state activities sponsored by the SEP as a result of the 1998-2000 memorandum of understanding. Another annex to the agreement was signed for 2000-2002, with no significant changes from the previous agreement. Information on the international agreement with Mexico has been added to the main Department of Education's website.[12]

Before 1990, Fulbright grants were awarded by the U.S. Information Agency and administered by a foreign service officer at the U.S. embassy in Mexico City. But no formal mechanism existed for supporting and expanding educational and cultural exchanges between Mexico and the United States, though the United States had these types of agreements with 40 other nations. In November 1990 Presidents Bush and Salinas signed an agreement to create the U.S.-Mexico Commission for Educational and Cultural Exchange. The entire Fulbright budget devoted to Mexico — a total of $2 million — became the first-year budget of the new organization. Mexico agreed to contribute $1 million as well. A 10-member board of directors was named jointly by the Mexican foreign secretary and the U.S. ambassador; six of the 10 members came from the private sector. Carlos Ornelas became the first executive director of the commission.

More than 150 grants were awarded during the first year of the new agreement. Besides the Fulbright funds, the commission

Table 5. SEP activities resulting from the 1998-2000 U.S.-Mexico memorandum of understanding.

National Projects
- Textbooks
- Special education meetings
- Binational commission
- Internet for adult education
- Fulbright scholarships
- Courses in Mexican universities
- Teacher exchanges
- Binational document
- *La Paloma* (a newspaper on education)
- Adult education for the border region
- Telesecundaria

Arizona
- Exchange of experts and materials
- Bilingual conference

California
- Telesecundaria
- Student exchange
- Bilingual teacher education program
- Program at CSU San Diego
- Teachers working in California

Colorado
- Adult education

Florida
- Exchange of specialists

Illinois
- Teachers in Chicago

Indiana
- Special program, "Mexicans in the 20th Century"
- Teacher exchange

Louisiana
- Post-graduate program

Michigan
- Training in the hotel industry

Missouri
- Careers in autos and electronics
- Scientific, technical, and cultural exchange

New York
- Culinary exchange

Oklahoma
- Program with University of Oklahoma

New Jersey
- Program with Educational Testing Service

New Mexico
- Telesecundaria

Pennsylvania
- Telesecundaria

Texas
- Exchanges in many universities and colleges
- Postgraduate work
- Telesecundaria

Utah
- Interchange in science

Virginia
- Interchange

received pledges that totaled $1 million from the Rockefeller Foundation, the Mexican National Council for Culture and the Arts, and the Bancomer Cultural Foundation for nonacademic cultural exchanges in such diverse fields as dance, translation, and library management. Research proposals in cultural scholarship were funded, as were conferences on a broad array of cultural themes. During 1998 about 500 grants were funded. Currently there is a Fulbright exchange program for secondary and community college teachers. Under this program, the U.S. educator works in Mexico for one semester, and then a Mexican teacher works in the United States for a semester. During the 1998-99 school year there were 21 Mexican citizens and 21 U.S. citizens involved in the program.[13]

In San Marcos, California families have benefited in 2001-02 from a pilot program sponsored by the Mexican government. The participants are learning to read and write in Spanish, and they are learning how to use the Internet. Textbooks and trained teachers at the primary and secondary level are provided by the SEP. The program is called *Plazas Communitarias e-Mexico*, and the program will be extended to Denver, Philadelphia, and El Paso.[14]

State Projects

State projects take many forms. Some evolve from border conferences; others are administered by private agencies under contract to the state. Sometimes foundations develop from the original state-funded project. It is impossible to list all of the cross-border programs that exist, but I will attempt to list the major ones dealing with literacy, teacher education, or student exchanges in the states of California, New Mexico, Arizona, and Texas.

According to the Mexican Foreign Service, 40% of the Mexicans living in the United States reside in California. This, coupled with the fact that Los Angeles is the second largest Spanish-speaking city in the world, provides the rationale for the state of California and some of its school districts to be involved in projects with Mexico.

In 1982 the Binational Program between Michoacán and California became a reality. The program simplifies the movement of migrants from the Mexican state of Michoacán to California and has funded research on the educational and social plight of international migrant children. In 1984 Deborah Mounts received funding for a study to track students who spent part of the year in French Camp, California, and the rest of the year in Villa Mendoza and Acuitzeramo, Michoacán. Her study was based on observations, teacher questionnaires, and family portraits. Mounts' findings about education were enlightening. The migrants followed traditional patterns that did not change from year to year. They spent about the same number of days in each country (184 in Mexico and 181 in the United States) with about the same number of potential school days (142 days in the United States and 140 days in Mexico). The school days in the United States were divided between summer school (46) and regular school (96). Each time the students moved from Mexico to the United States or the reverse, they had to take placement tests, integrate into an ongoing program, become accustomed to new texts, and learn to function with new teachers and classmates. Students tended to be placed in classes and programs below their ability levels.[15]

In 1986 the Binational Program introduced the "Binational Transfer Document" to help correct these problems. As of 1996, 10 U.S. states were participating in the Binational Program. To register, the student must have a birth certificate and a transfer document validated with the binational seal. Students with proper documentation are accepted any time of the year in the Mexican school and are placed at the same grade level in the U.S. school. No examinations are required. If a student does not have proper documentation, an initial assessment is free; and this assessment is administered in local offices, instead of at the state level. The transfer document also carries a student's grades. Since 1 January 1996 the "Binational Transfer Document" has been in use in every Mexican state.

The California State Department of Education did not fund the Binational Program during the 1998-99 school year, and thus participation focused on the regional, rather than the state, level. Currently, there is a coordinator of the program at the state level.

On 26 June 1991 a binational conference on literacy and adult education was held in Los Angeles. The purpose of the conference was to help the Los Angeles School District study the problems and education needs of the Mexican population that it serves. This conference focused on teaching skills, materials, evaluation, staff training, and problems faced by literacy programs. A series of reports and several proposals for inter-institutional collaboration emerged from the discussions. Mexico sent representatives from the regional center of Adult Education and Literacy for Latin America (CREFAL), the National Institute for Adult Education (INEA), the Education Investigations Department of IPN, Northern Border College of Mexico, the Chihuahua centers for education studies, the Iberoamerican University, and the National Pedagogic University.[16]

In August 1993 the Mexican Secretary of Education signed an agreement with the Los Angeles Unified School District to provide Mexican schoolteachers to work in bilingual classrooms. The teachers returned to Mexico after working for two years in Los Angeles.

In 1998 the program between Mexico and Los Angeles was a three-year program. After teachers apply for the program, administrators from the United States interview them. If they have the necessary English skills and met the requirements established by the Commission for Teacher Credentialing, they are issued nonrenewable credentials and work in the school district, receiving the same pay as a U.S. citizen would receive with this credential.[17]

The California State Department of Education decided to expand the program. During the 2001-02 school year, 74 Mexican teachers were serving in major California cities, including San Jose, Lynnwood, Los Angeles, and Fresno.[18]

In New Mexico, in cooperation with the Southwest Educational Development Laboratory (SEDL), a teacher exchange program was developed between the Mexican states of Nuevo León and

Guanajuato. Teachers spent two weeks in both countries, living with the host-country teacher and working in the classrooms. Several binational border conferences were held, and from these efforts a binational school was created in Columbus, New Mexico.

The history of this binational school is very interesting. Since 1949 Mexicans have been crossing the border to attend schools in the Deming Public School District in New Mexico. In fact, the superintendent ordered the school buses to park on the U.S. side of the border crossing so that the students would not have to walk on a two-lane road to the school. When NAFTA came into existence, the population of Palomas, Mexico, grew from 1,000 people to 10,000 people. With the help of SEDL, discussions took place and the binational school was established. Columbus was chosen because the town did not have enough students to support a junior/senior high school, and students were bused the 32 miles to Deming for education above the elementary school level. The new bilingual school served 890 students, 500 from Mexico and 390 from the Columbus area. Mexican teachers came to the school and taught Spanish to the students while teachers from the United States went to the Mexican schools to teach English. There were many meetings and social events to facilitate the exchange of ideas between the Mexican and the U.S. teachers. The school lasted from the 1995-96 school year to the 1997-98 school year. Because of the massive importation of drugs and the resulting border restrictions to enter the United States, the border crossings became too time-consuming for the Mexican students; and the binational school had to close. Currently, the school district is looking for funding to support an interactive computer program between the schools in Palomas and Columbus.[19]

The Arizona-Mexico Commission and the Arizona-Sonora Commission established education institutes, published a yearly magazine called *Horizontes*, and facilitated the exchange of students in elementary and middle school. In 1981 the Hands Across the Border project started as an educational exchange between the Palomino School District in Arizona and Arizpe, Sonora. On

4 March 1999 I talked to officials in the district — 50 students had just arrived from Mexico. The Mexican students (grade 5) would live with students in Arizona for the weekend. They attended a multicultural assembly on Thursday night, and on Friday they took a bus tour to Tombstone, Arizona. Friday night was spent with the families, and on Saturday the students returned to Mexico. The situation would reverse in the fall, and the Mexican fifth-graders would become the hosts for students from Arizona. Parents, teachers, and community members were part of the trip. In 1986 the program was expanded into a private foundation so that students throughout the United States could participate.

During the 1998-99 school year, between four thousand and five thousand students participated in exchanges in 65 schools in Arizona and one school in New Mexico. They obtained money through fundraising at the schools and through mini-grants. The trips averaged $2,000 to $3,000 for each of the 20 to 30 students in the groups. In areas where the program was new, there were adult exchanges to plan the trips.[20]

The state of Arizona allows 50 Mexican students from the state of Sonora to attend community college in Arizona with preferential fees. In addition, 50 Arizona students can study at Sonoran universities for reduced fees. The state has an agreement to donate computer equipment to education institutions at all levels in Sonora, and so far more than 100 computers have been donated.

In Texas the state cooperates and provides partial funding for the Center for Research on Education for Students Placed At Risk (CRESPAR) program from Johns Hopkins University. One of their programs, Success for All, provides help in preschool, elementary, and secondary schools through professional development training, tutoring, and family support. The Success for All program is being used in Juárez, Mexico; and there is professional development training throughout the state of Chihuahua. A private foundation based in Juárez funded a 120-hour training course for principals in Chihuahua.[21]

In *Children of La Frontera*, Margarita Calderón talks about the Leadership Enhancement Academy for binational education.

Principals, assistant principals, and coordinators from El Paso and Ciudad Juárez worked together to create this academy. The goal of the organization is to cultivate relationships, provide professional development on both sides of the border, develop an integrated approach to address the multiple aspects of bilingual education, and conduct research and evaluation.[22]

Another project described in *Children of La Frontera* is the Border Colloquy Project. This project was done in cooperation with the Southwest Educational Development Laboratory (SEDL). In March 1994, SEDL organized a series of meetings with local and state education officials. Following is the vision statement of the group, which was developed by participants in the colloquy at Austin, Texas, 1-2 August 1994:

> We in the Mexico-United States border region, looking toward education in the year 2010, consider our children to be our most precious resource. Therefore, every individual has the right to equal educational opportunities through which she/he will develop self-esteem, dignity, cultural pride, understanding of others, and the capacity to become a positive, contributing member of society.
>
> To respond to the needs of this international, multilingual multicultural community, we will have a binational educational system that is open, flexible, integrated, of high quality and adapted to the region's common needs in an atmosphere of community. Recognizing the family as critical in the child's development, this system will offer health and human services and family education. It will include staff development and programs teaching environmental improvement, international understanding, cultural and moral traditions and values and the skills to compete in a global economic society. It will use technology resources and multicultural multilingual strategies.[23]

As often happens, the individuals responsible for this project no longer work for SEDL, and the new management has a different focus. Consequently SEDL no longer sponsors the Border Colloquy Project.

On 17 June 2001 Texas Governor Rick Perry signed a bill that allows immigrants who have lived in Texas at least three years and earned a GED or high school diploma from a Texas school to attend the state's universities on in-state tuition levels, instead of paying international fees. To qualify for the reduced fees, students must sign an affidavit stating that they will apply for permanent resident status when they are eligible. During the 2001-02 school year, about 3,000 students were eligible to attend the university under this bill.[24] The California legislature has passed a bill and the governor signed it into law allowing in-state tuition for undocumented aliens who have graduated from California high schools.

A total of 17 states (or agencies within the states) have agreements with Mexico. The states include Arizona, California, Colorado, Florida, Illinois, Indiana, Louisiana, Michigan, Missouri, New Jersey, New Mexico, New York, Oklahoma, Pennsylvania, Texas, Utah, and Virginia. The programs range from simple teacher exchanges or providing bilingual teachers to the use of the Mexican *telesecundaria* program by satellite.

Private Agencies

One Stop Immigration is a community-based nonprofit organization that started in 1972. In 1975 it began to work on legalization and immigration issues. The major funding source is the city of Los Angeles. In 1987 the group applied to the California State Department of Education for permission to offer classes in history and English as a second language (ESL) in order to prepare people for the federal amnesty program. However, because many of the students were illiterate in Spanish, the program had to be expanded beyond its original scope.

During April 1990 the INEA provided training for staff members of One Stop Immigration. In August 1990 Mexico shipped seven trailerloads of INEA materials to Los Angeles (153,715 elementary and secondary books for use with adults). Teachers came from Mexico to teach the One Stop Immigration staff to use the materials.

106

Since 1988 One Stop has served more than 87,000 people. In August 1992 about 9,000 people attended their schools in 21 service centers located throughout California. After completing the primaria or secundaria program, people applied to take the test that earned them a Mexican primary or secondary certificate. In 1992 some 3,000 people enrolled in the primaria program, and approximately 30 smaller agencies in the Los Angeles area used the Mexican materials.[25]

Because of cuts in funding, the program recently has been drastically reduced. The new goals are adult education, ESL training, and citizenship education. They have helped 50,000 people to become legal residents and 25,000 people to become citizens of the United States. Currently, they are not using the Mexican materials, and a very small percentage of their students are illiterate. Most come to the United States with at least a fourth-grade education from Mexico.[26]

Another small program in California is the Los Niños program. Each year they send between 12 and 16 interns to teach first- and second-grade classes in the primary schools of Tijuana. The interns work for six weeks during the summer, and they live with Mexican families in Tijuana.

In 1981 nine U.S. universities in the Southwest (University of Texas at Austin, University of Texas at El Paso, University of New Mexico, New Mexico State University, University of Arizona, Arizona State University, San Diego State University, University of California Los Angeles, and Stanford University) formed PROFMEX (the Consortium for Research on Mexico) to find mechanisms to enhance communication and collaboration among researchers on contemporary issues in U.S.-Mexican relations. PROFMEX was joined by ANUIES (Asociación Nacional de Universidades e Institutos de Educación Superior). Together the two organizations sponsor research, hold meetings, print a monograph series, print a newsletter, and offer advice on border issues. PROFMEX includes a worldwide membership of 105 universities, organizations, and think tanks, as well as more than 700 individual members in countries throughout the world.

In 1992 PROFMEX launched a computer network, "PROFMEXIS," with the support of the Ford Foundation. PROFMEXIS gave network users customized e-mail communication, database access, and a file-transfer capability. The communications center in Mexico is the Centro de Tecnología e Información, with the database and communication facilities provided by the University of Mexico. The permanent home for the database in the United States is at the Austin campus of the University of Texas. Through this system, scholars have customized access to the holdings of major research libraries and a diversity of public databases in the social and natural sciences. PROFMEXIS has evolved and set new goals to provide lists of resources and Internet links useful to Mexico public policy researchers. [27]

The International Reading Association publishes a journal, titled *Lectura y Vida*, to which Mexican authors contribute articles. At this time, the organization has a local council in Guadalajara and another in Nuevo León. Individuals from the Guadalajara chapter participated in a presentation at the International Reading Association's 44th annual convention at San Diego in May 1999. At the first conference of the Guadalajara Chapter in Guadalajara, researchers and educators from many U.S. and Mexican states attended. The editor of *Lectura y Vida* from Argentina also was present.

Another agency is the Mexican and American Solidarity Foundation. This foundation is governed by a binational board of directors, including representatives of the National Council of La Raza, Intercultural Development Research Association, El Colegio de la Frontera Norte, University of Texas, Televisa, Univision, American GI Forum, National Clearinghouse for Bilingual Education, Arizona State University, the secretaries of Public Education and Foreign Relations in Mexico, U.S. Hispanic Chamber of Commerce, and the League of United Latin American Citizens. The organization focuses on a wide range of activities concerning Mexicans on both sides of the border. One program of particular interest is called "Teaching Certificates in

Bilingual-Bicultural Education for Mexican Teachers living in the U.S." The program offers a bachelor's degree in two and a half years for Mexican teachers who are legal residents of California. The program is at the California State University at Long Beach; and in 1998, 27 of the 30 participants graduated.

The Intercultural Development Research Association is sponsoring Project Alianza, which is a teacher preparation and leadership development initiative. This project is conducted in cooperation with the Mexican and American Solidarity Foundation. In five years, the project will enable 200 teachers to teach and become leaders on education issues in bilingual, binational, and bicultural settings. They plan to target bilingual teacher aides, students in traditional bilingual teacher preparation programs, and Mexican-trained primaria teachers who are legal residents of the United States. This will be accomplished at seven universities in Mexico and the United States, and participating school districts will create opportunities for new teachers to have preparation laboratories and practice.

Implications

The border between the United States and Mexico is never wider than a river, and there are large Spanish-speaking communities on both sides of that river. Because of socioeconomic conditions, Mexicans in the United States are, as a group, not very prosperous. Both governments and many private agencies have recognized this condition. A truly international effort to improve the lives of Mexicans who live in the United States is now under way.

In pursuing literacy for all members of the family, cultural exchanges and increased teacher training have been shown to be effective ways of educating this group. The use of Mexican textbooks and the incentive of a Mexican diploma — coupled with mutual attempts to understand education in both countries — are paying off. As education becomes more important to the family, the economic level of the family will rise and the younger children will stay in school longer. In addition, U.S. educators are learning from their Mexican counterparts how to handle the unique strengths of the Mexican students. The prospects are encouraging.

Notes

1. "Most Migrants Are Neither Illiterate Nor Poor," *The News,* Mexico City, 4 July 2001. http://www.thenewsnewsmexico.com
2. Carlos Gonzalez Gutierrez, "The Mexican Diaspora in California," in *The California Mexico Connection*, edited by Abraham Lowenthal and Katrina Burgess (Stanford, Calif.: Stanford University Press, 1993).
3. Alan Riding, *Distant Neighbors* (New York: Random House, 1984), p. 475.
4. Robert Miller, "Mexican Immigrants Can Achieve in U.S. Schools," *CATESOL Journal* 4, no.1 (1991): 91-96.
5. Roger Díaz de Cossio, "Mexico and the Mexican Origin Population in the U.S." Report. (Mexico City: Secretaría de Relaciones Exteriores, 24 January 1992).
6. Interview with Sofia and Graciela Orozco, Mexico City, 15 June 1992.
7. *La Paloma* (Mexico City: Secretaría de Relaciones Exteriores, September-December 1993).
8. Interview with Sofia Orozco, 7 July 1997.
9. *La Paloma* (Mexico City: Secretaría de Relaciones Exteriores, January-February 1991).
10. "Immersion Courses for Bilingual Teachers in the United States," Brochure (Mexico: Comunidades Mexicanas en El Extranjero, n.d.).
11. *Report on the Border Conference on Education, October 6-8, 1991* (Washington, D.C.: U.S. Department of Education, 1991).
12. Telephone interview with Rafael Nevarez, U.S. Department of Education, 6 November 2001.
13. Telephone Interview with USIA officials, 1 March 1999.
14. Dirección General de Communicación Social, "Se Inaugura la Primera Plaza Comunitaria en San Marcos, CA." http://www.srl. gob.mx/d-cs/b-204.htm

15. Deborah Mounts, *The Binational Child* (California: State Department of Education, Department of Migrant Education, 1986).
16. *La Paloma* (Mexico City: Secretaría de Relaciones Exteriores, October-December 1991).
17. Telephone interview with Carlos de la Torre, Secretaría de Educación Pública representative in Los Angeles, 2 March 1999.
18. Telephone interview with Edda Caraballo, Coordinator of the Migrant Education Binational Program, 6 November 2001.
19. Telephone interview with Carlos Viramontes, Superintendent of the Deming Public Schools, 2 March 1999.
20. Telephone interview with Judy Freeman of the Hands Across the Border Foundation, 4 March 1999.
21. Telephone interview with Margarita Calderon, 8 March 1999.
22. Margarita Calderon, "Bilingual, Bicultural and Binational Cooperative Learning Communities for Students and Teachers," in *Children of La Frontera*, edited by Judith Flores (Charleston, W.V.: Clearinghouse on Rural Education and Small Schools, 1996).
23. Betty Mace-Matluck and M. Boethel, "Exploring Binational Educational Issues: A Report from the Border Colloquy Project," in *Children of La Frontera*, edited by Judith Flores (Charleston, W.V.: Clearinghouse on Rural Education and Small Schools, 1996).
24. "Gov't Praises Texas Law for In-State Tuition," *The News*, 19 June 2001, p. 2.
25. Telephone interview with Angelina Flores, August 1992.
26. Telephone interview with Mario Evilla, Controller, One Stop Immigration, 26 February 1999.
27. PROFMEX, San Diego State University, Institute for Regional Studies of the Californias, *Mexico Policy News* (Fall 1991).

CHAPTER SEVEN
FUTURE TRENDS

I began this work with a quotation from the director of a primary school: "We Mexicans have particular ideas about the world; we value truth, demand respect, honor, and we want to be consulted about things that concern us. Also, we have strong feelings about our country, our flag, our national hymn, and our history." Throughout the book, I have tried to honor the concepts in the quotation by showing from a historical perspective the tremendous obstacles that Mexican educators have worked to overcome. In public education, teacher training, bilingual education, adult education, special education, and outreach programs to the United States, Mexican educators and politicians have been working to improve their system of education and to improve and expand literacy instruction. I have watched scores of individuals at all levels working very hard to improve the quality of education. At the ministry level, there seems to be impatience because these individuals want rapid improvement. Frequently because of cultural and social issues, the progress has been very slow. But in general there is no denying that the system has improved, and more Mexican citizens today are receiving a high-quality education than ever before.

Several trends suggest a positive outlook for Mexican education. These trends include a lower birthrate, increasing preschool and basic education, more education opportunities for indigenous people, improved adult education, greater teacher effectiveness, and better relationships with the United States. Of these, perhaps the most important trend is the lower birthrate. By 2006 the estimated school-aged population will have dropped by 3%, and by 2010 it will have dropped 10%. Because of this decline, the focus

113

is on repairing facilities instead of building new ones. Mexico's citizens realize that the new economy requires both parents to work, and they are moving to the *turno completo* schools, where the students attend from 8:00 a.m. to 3:00 p.m. As school populations dip, the morning and afternoon sessions in the city schools are being combined into one school. With this change has come money to modernize the schools, install computer labs, and provide more resources. Because more money is available, the *Escuelas de Culidad* program is popular. Schools are applying for these grants to modernize facilities and to buy more equipment.

When I began this study in 1978-79, there were 5,535 preschools, compared to 68,136 for the 1998-99 school year, only 20 years later. There were 699,000 students in 1978-79, compared to 3,013,500 today. The Mexican government also is enlarging the preschool program to help indigenous people. In the future, preschools will continue to have a high priority.

On the other end of the K-12 spectrum, completion of secondary school and acquisition of functional literacy are extremely important to an industrialized society. A law passed in 1992 makes secondary education mandatory; all students must attend school from first grade to ninth grade. Still, at this point, this is not realistic. In 1978-79 there were 2,505,200 students in the secondary schools. Now, there are 5,084,300. There were 7,711 schools in 1978-79, and today there are 26,743.

The government also is stressing the importance of science and math. In the secondary curriculum, the general courses of math and science were replaced with specific subject courses (biology, physics, chemistry) and the government is purchasing computers for secondary schools. Also, the government has received international grants to improve science instruction at the secondary level. This trend will continue with more schools, and more students attending them. The SEP is working to meet the demand for the functional literacy required by Mexico's new trade status in the world.

The primary-school dropout rate has been a constant problem, and resources are committed to help solve the problem. In 1978-

114

79 the dropout rate was 54%; now it is 15%. The dropout rate is not balanced; in the richer states, more students stay in school than in the poorer states. Over the years, various programs have been devised to address this problem, such as combining fifth and sixth grades for students who failed fifth grade, special education programs, afternoon programs for dropouts, and special classes for students who failed first or second grade. Parents have become involved with writing school mission statements; and in at least one school, former graduates are used to convince students to stay in school.

Indigenous education is very important to the Mexican government. When I began this study in 1978 only the *Instituto Nacional Indigenista* was supplying education programs to this group. By 1982 a new dirección in the SEP was handling the education needs of the indigenous people. The dirección provided services for 244,000 people in 1978, and in 1989 it provided services to more than one million people. These services were provided through cash grants to keep girls in school, to produce radio programs, and to fund special schools. As seen from the comments of teachers who work with indigenous people, there is a tremendous amount of frustration. Students often have to walk long distances to attend school, and many do not have much to eat. This will continue to be an area of focus because the indigenous people are the poorest citizens and are the most marginalized group in the country.

Adult education is another area of concern. In the past, literacy campaigns were held to increase literacy. Now there is a permanent agency to handle this problem. Much is being done in cooperation with industry, government, and the military. The program has been redesigned to make it practical; and the effort by the military, in particular, is paying off. Through literacy training of 18-year-olds and workplace training, the problem of adult illiteracy is being reduced. This agency is very creative, and more innovative programs will be forthcoming.

Increasing the effectiveness of the teaching staff is another objective of the government. When this study began, teachers needed a total of only 13 years of education to work in the primary school. Now they need 16 years. The Universidad Pedagógica Nacional (UPN) and teacher centers help teachers receive more training. Many teachers attend courses on Saturdays and during vacations. In addition, teachers do not make enough to live comfortably, which means that many teachers have to work two shifts. As teachers move up in the Carerra Magistrial, they will make more money; and this will help to attract more qualified people to the profession.

The decentralization of the school system has been in the works since the de la Madrid administration. Officially, the purpose is to make schools more responsive to the public by transferring the administration of the schools to the states. As states assume more responsibility for the school system, the schools will become more responsive to local needs.

The Program for Citizens Abroad is a first step in organizing Mexican nationals in the United States. It has been successful because the program has the support of the president, and there are people committed to breaking down the barriers between Mexico and the United States. Educators in the United States are searching for ways to help Mexican students. There will be more programs, not fewer, as the U.S. federal government, the states, and individual school districts discover the value of Mexican textbooks and materials. Also, as more Mexican-American politicians are elected in the United States, programs with Mexico will become more politically feasible. After a long period of "Mexico bashing" by politicians, more cooperation and sensitivity seem to be evolving. For example, Congress is contemplating a guest-worker program. Both governments are examining means to reduce the deaths on the border, and Texas and California now allow immigrants to pay in-state tuition at their colleges and universities.

On the negative side, many education journals in the United States see Mexicans in U.S. schools as a regional issue, and they do not focus on this group. Also, some of the more traditional programs offered by national education organizations do not work with Mexicans. For example, some organizations believe that Mexicans are in the United States only for economic reasons; thus no matter how much we restructure or reform our curriculum, we cannot change the economic fact that students drop out of school to go to work or to support family members who do not work. Many of these national organizations also do not see Mexico as a "status country," and so they often ignore the issues that involve educating Mexican children. As Mexicans migrate to more U.S. states and as Mexican-American politicians gain power, this situation should change.

The opportunity has never been greater for an expanded education relationship between Mexico and the United States. Cooperation will produce benefits both north and south of the Rio Grande.

BIBLIOGRAPHY

Acuerdo Nacional Para la Modernización de la Educación Básica. Mexico: Secretaría de Educación Pública, 18 May 1992.

Alvarez Garcia, Isaias. *A Search for New Alternatives in the Educación of Mexico's Future Primary School Teachers.* Boston: Harvard University Press, 1983.

Articulo 41 Comentado de la Ley General de Educación. Cuadernos de Integración Educativa No.2. Mexico: Dirección General de Educación Especial, 1994.

Avance Programáticos. Mexico: Secretaría de Educación Pública, 1993.

Blair, Evelyn. "Educational Movements in Mexico, 1821 to 1836." Doctoral dissertation, University of Texas, 1941.

Calderón, Margarita. "Bilingual, Bicultural and Binational Cooperative Learning Communities for Students and Teachers." In *Children of La Frontera,* edited by Judith Flores, Charleston, W.V.: Clearinghouse on Rural Education and Small Schools, 1996.

Campos Esquerra, Roy. "La Sociedad Juzga a los Maestros." *Educación 2001* (May 1998): 27-33.

"Capacitación a Directores de Escuelas en el D.F." *Educación 2001* (August 1996): 11-14.

Cheetham, Nicolas. *Mexico: A Short History.* New York: Thomas Y. Crowell, 1971.

Comisión Nacional de los Libros de Texto Gratuitos. http://www.conaliteg.gob.mx/cuadro1998.html

Compendio Estaíistico-Gráfico de Educación, 1997. Mexico: Instituto Nacional de Estadística Geograpfía e Informática, 1998.

Declaración de Salamanca de Principios, Politica y Practica para las Necesidades Educativas Especiales. Cuadernos de Integración Educativa No.3. Mexico: Dirección General de Educación Especial, 1994.

de la Garza, Paul. "Teachers Strike Spotlights Mexico's Education Failures." *Chicago Tribune*, 22 May 1997, p. 8.

119

Díaz de Cossio, Roger. "Mexico and the Mexican Origin Population in the U.S." Report. Mexico City: Secretaría de Relaciones Exteriores, January 1992.

Downing, John. *Comparative Reading: Cross National Studies of Behavior and Processes in Reading and Writing.* New York: Macmillian, 1973.

"Educación Indigena." *Educación 2001* (December 1995): 6-17.

"Education Secretary: Only One Percent of Indigenous Children Study at Universities." *The News*, Mexico City, 27 October 2001. http://www.thenewsmexico.com/noticia.asp?id=11515

"Entrevista con Jésus Liceaga." *Educación 2001* (March 1999): 12.

Estadísticas de Educación. Cuaderno Numero 6. Mexico: Instituto Nacional de Estadística Geograpfía e Informática, 2000.

Farfán, Enrique, and Amador, Pilar. "La Enseñanza de la Lecto Escritura." *Educación 2001* (February 1998): 25-28.

Fashola, Olatokumbo; Slavin, Robert; et al. "Effective Programs for Latino Students in Elementary and Middle Schools." http://www.ncbe.gwu/edu/

Fisher, Maria. *Latino Education Status and Prospects: State of Hispanic America, 1998.* Washington, D.C.: National Council of La Raza, 1998.

Gill, Clark. *Education in a Changing Mexico.* Washington, D.C.: U.S. Government Printing Office, 1957.

González Gutiérrez, Carlos. "The Mexican Diaspora in California." In *The California-Mexico Connection*, edited by Abraham F. Lowenthal and Katrina Burgess. Stanford, Calif.: Stanford University Press, 1993.

"Gov't Praises Texas Law for In-State Tuition," *The News*, 19 June 2001, p. 2.

Gray, William. *The Teaching of Reading and Writing.* Paris: UNESCO, 1956.

Guzmán Cota, Marcelino. "Perfil del Estudiante de Normal." *Educación 2001* (September 1995): 22-24.

Haydee Estevez, Etty. "La Lucha Contra el Rezago." *Educación 2001* (January 1996): 53-58.

Hernandez, Julio Minjares. "El Método Minjares." In *La Enseñanza de la Lectura por Medio de los Métodos Globales.* Mexico: Editorial Pax, 1984.

"Hunger Strikers Gives Teachers' Side of Story." *The News*, 31 January 1999.

"Immersion Courses for Bilingual Teachers in the United States." Brochure. Mexico: Communidades Mexicanas en el Extranjero, n.d.

Informe de Labores, 1987-88. Mexico: Secretaría de Educación Pública, 1988.

Informe de Labores, 1997-98. Mexico: Secretaría de Educación Pública, 1998.

Instituto Nacional para la Educación de los Adultos. *Aprendio Juntos.* Mexico City: Secretaría de Educación Pública, n.d.

Intercultural Development Research Association, February 1998 Newsletter. http://www.idra/Newslettr/1998

Ivie, Stanley. "A Comparison in Educational Philosophy: Jose Vasconcelos and John Dewey." *Comparative Education Review* 10 (October 1966): 404.

Instituto Nacional para la Educación de los Adultos. *Marco Operativo del Programa.* Mexico: Secretaría de Educación Pública, 1997.

La Educación Especial en México. Mexico: Dirección General de Educación Especial, 1981.

La Integración Educativa como Fundamento de la Calidad del Sistema de Educación Basica para Todos. Cuadernos de Integración Educativa No.5. Mexico: Dirección General de Educación Especial, 1994.

Lange, Jason. "Government to Open Books on Tlatelolco Massacre." *The News,* Mexico City, 3 October 2001. http://www.novedades.com.mx/national.htm

"Las Escuelas Particulares En La Educación." *Educación 2001* (February 1996).

Leonard, Mary Joan. "Anti-illiteracy Campaigns in Mexico, 1944-46." Master's thesis, University of California at Berkeley, 1958.

Libro Para el Maestro. Mexico: Secretaría de Educación Pública, 1981.

Lira, Jennifer. "Aprender a Leer" *Educación 2001* (January 1999): 28-31.

Mace-Matluck, B., and Boethel, M. "Exploring Binational Educational Issues: A Report from the Border Colloquy Project." In *Children of La Frontera,* edited by Judith Flores. Charleston, W.V.: Clearinghouse on Rural Education and Small Schools, 1996.

Merrill, T.A., and Miró, R. *Mexico: A Country Study.* Washington, D.C.: U.S. Government Printing Office, 1997.

Miller, Robert. "Public Primary School Education in Mexico: A Focus on Reading Instruction in Mexico City." Doctoral dissertation, University of San Francisco, 1980.

Miller, Robert. "Mexican Immigrants Can Achieve in U.S. Schools." *CATESOL Journal* 4, no.1 (1991): 91-96.

Modiano, Nancy. "Reading Comprehension in the National Language: A Comparative Study of Bilingual and All Spanish Approaches to Reading Instruction in Selected Indian Schools in the Highland of Chiapas, Mexico." Doctoral dissertation, New York University, 1966.

Morrow, L.; Tracey, D.; and Maxwell, Caterina. *A Survey of Family Literacy in the United States*. Newark, Del.: International Reading Association, 1995.

Moore, Molly. "Mexican Waifs Ply Meanest of Streets." *Washington Post*, 10 December 1996, p. A1.

"Most Migrants Are Neither Illiterate Nor Poor." *The News*, Mexico City, 4 July 2001. http://www.thenewsnewsmexico.com

Mounts, Deborah. *The Bi-National Child*. Sacramento: California Department of Education, Department of Migrant Education, 1986.

Olsen, Laurie. *Crossing the Schoolhouse Border: Immigrant Students and the California Public Schools*. San Francisco: California Tomorrow, 1988.

Olsen, Laurie. *The Unfinished Journey: Restructuring Schools in a Diverse Society*. San Francisco: California Tomorrow, 1994.

Padgett, Vincent. *The Mexican Political System*. Atlanta: Houghton-Mifflin, 1976.

"Pasado, Presente y Futuro de la UPN." *Educación 2001* (September 1997): 28-38.

Plan y Program de Educación y Capacitación de la Mujer Indigena. Mexico: Dirección General de Educación Indigena, 1988.

Primaria: Plan y Programas de Estudio. Mexico: Secretaría de Educación Pública, 1993.

Proyecto General para la Educación Especial en Mexico. Cuadernos de Integración Educativa No.1. Mexico: Secretaría de Educación Pública, Dirección General de Educación Especial, 1994.

Proyecto General para la Educación Especial Pautas de Organización. Cuadernos de Integración Educativa No. 6. Mexico: Secretaría de Educación Pública, Dirección General de Educación Especial, 1994.

"¿Quien Gobierna la Educación en México?" *Educación 2001* (March 1997): 6-12.

"¿Quien Gobierna la Educación en México?" *Educación 2001* (April 1997): 8-14.

Report on the Border Conference on Education, October 6-8, 1991. Washington, D.C.: U.S. Department of Education, 1991.

Riding, Allan. *Distant Neighbors.* New York: Random House, 1984.

Rosas Barrera, Federico. "Mexico Indigena: Un Perfil Estadístico." *Educación 2001* (December 1995): 32-35.

Rosas Barrera, Frederico. "Vista Familiar." *Educación 2001* (January 1996): 51-52.

"Se Inaugura la Primera Plaza Comunitaria en San Marcos, CA." Mexico: Dirección General de Communicación Social. http://www.srl.gob.mx/d-cs/b-204.htm

Secada, Walter; Chavez-Chavez, Rudolfo; et al. *No More Excuses: The Final Report of the Hispanic Dropout Project.* Washington, D.C.: Department of Education, 1998.

"16,000 Indigenous Children Kept Out of School for Lacking a Birth Certificate." *The News,* Mexico City, 12 October 2001. http:://the newsmexico.com

Smith, James. "Changing Demographics Create Opportunities for Fox." *The News*, Mexico City, 24 September 2000. http://www.novedades.com.mx national.htm

"Teacher's Union Accepts Pay Raise." *The News*, Mexico City, 16 May 2001, p. 2.

"The Textbook Controversy." *Mexico Journal*, 3 October 1988, p. 19.

Thonis, Eleanor. *Literacy for America's Spanish Speaking Children.* Newark, Del.: International Reading Association, 1976.

Unidad de Servicios de Apoyo a la Educación Regular (USAER). *Cuadernos de Integración Educativa No.4.* Mexico: Secretaría de Educación Pública, Dirección General de Educación Especial, 1994.

Wilson, Irma. *Mexico: A Century of Educational Thought.* West Port, Conn.: Greenwood Press, 1974.